HAL MORGAN
AND DAN SYMMES

Vermilion • London
and Little, Brown • Boston

Picture Credits

ISBN: 0-316-58283-2 (pbk), 0-316-58284-0 (hc)
Library of Congress Catalog Card Number: 82-82781

Published simultaneously in Canada by Little, Brown & Company (Canada) Limited

Design and production by Steam Press, Cambridge, Massachusetts

PRINTED IN THE UNITED STATES OF AMERICA

CONTENTS

9   DAWN OF THE THIRD DIMENSION
How 3-D Started and How It Works

25   REELS TO REALISTS
Stereo Photography Comes of Age

53   HOLLYWOOD TAKES THE PLUNGE
The Movies Go 3-D

107   SUPERMAN BREAKS LOOSE
Comic Books Join the Charge

155   THE BIG SLEEP
3-D Since 1955

165   Chronology of Three-Dimensional
Motion Pictures

170   Chronology of Three-Dimensional
Comic Books

172   For More Information

173   Acknowledgments

174   Index

AMAZING 3-D

1.
DAWN OF THE THIRD DIMENSION

How 3-D Started and How It Works

Welcome to the world of depth and illusion, where caves stretch into distant darkness, meteors shoot from the page, and movie stars are utterly embraceable. Using the glasses from the first page of this book—and following the instructions printed there—you will be able to see in these orange and blue pictures the alluring effects of graphics in the third dimension.

Our aim is to give an illustrated history of the 3-D renaissance of the 1950s, so we have limited our treatment of earlier and later aspects of the subject to the essentials and to a few key reproductions. If you find you want to know more about something we touch on, the bibliography at the back of the book may be helpful.

3-D, despite its apparent novelty, claims a long and colorful heritage, stretching back as far as ancient Greece. Euclid laid out the principles of binocular vision long before there was a satisfactory method of making stereoscopic pictures. He demonstrated that the left and right eyes each see a slightly different image of the same object or scene and that it is the merging of these images that creates the perception of depth. You can see this for yourself by holding your finger up at arm's length. If you look past your finger at an object across the room, and close first one eye, then the other, you will see that the position of the finger changes from eye to eye. When you focus your eyes on your finger, the two images merge, and you perceive that your finger is closer to you than the wall of your room. Your eyes note much smaller differences when you observe objects only slightly varying distances apart, and still smaller differences when you study the roundness or volume of an object such as

OPPOSITE PAGE: Clifford Calverly poised on one foot over the Whirlpool Rapids at Niagara Falls, 1893. BELOW: As Euclid theorized, depth perception relies on the difference between

what the two eyes see. If you look at a distant object past your upraised finger, your finger will appear double. By fusing the double image you perceive depth.

 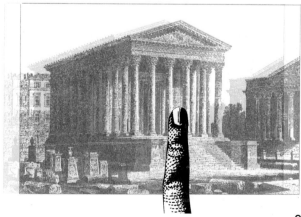

Sir Charles Wheatstone, inventor
of the stereoscope

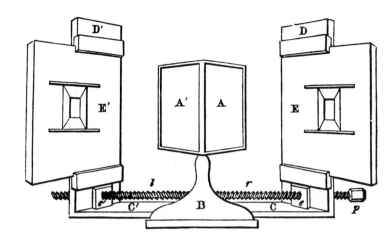

The Wheatstone stereoscope used angled mirrors (A) to reflect
the stereoscopic drawings (E) toward the viewer's eyes.

your finger. This same principle lies behind the 3-D illustrations in this book. If, with the glasses on, you close first one eye, then the other, you will see that different parts of the pictures are shifted to the left or right for each eye. By fusing the pictures, your eyes give you the illusion of seeing real depth.

After Euclid others theorized about binocular vision in more detail, among them Galen, Porta, and Aguilonius, and in the sixteenth century the Florentine painter Jacopo Chimenti experimented with stereoscopic drawing. A pair of Chimenti's drawings, which seem to have been made for stereoscopic viewing, are in the Wicar Museum in Lille.

Further progress in 3-D did not come until 1838, the year Sir Charles Wheatstone invented the reflecting, or mirror, stereoscope. To demonstrate his invention Wheatstone produced a series of simple paired drawings rendered as if seen by the left and right eyes. His device was bulky and his drawings crude, but together they did produce a three-dimensional effect.

The introduction of daguerreotypy in 1839 gave impetus to some rapid improvements. In 1844 a technique for taking stereoscopic photographs was demonstrated in Germany, and in Scotland David Brewster invented a much smaller and handier viewing device than Wheatstone's. In Brewster's system the mirrors were replaced with prismatic lenses. This allowed the pictures to be placed directly in front of the viewer rather than out to the sides, as with the Wheatstone viewing mechanism.

Stereoscopic photographs became the rage. France led the way, and England followed after Queen Victoria took a fancy to the stereoscope at the 1851 Crystal Palace Exposition. The United States trailed for some years, but in 1862 the Boston-designed Holmes stereoscope appeared and soon dominated the world market, establishing this country as a center of stereoscopic activity. The Holmes viewer, the handiwork of Oliver Wendell Holmes and Joseph Bates, became the standard stereoscopic instrument for decades, and it is still being produced in limited quantity.

BELOW, LEFT TO RIGHT: The Brewster stereoscope; an early Holmes viewer; a pair of later Holmes viewers, one on a parlor stand

COLBY BROTHERS & COMPANY.

ABOVE: Basket weaving in Waterbury, Vermont, about 1870, printed as a stereo card

BELOW: The same view printed for viewing with red and blue glasses

During the 1870s the stereoscope and its accompanying box of stereoscopic views grew to be almost as familiar a fixture in homes throughout the world as the television is today. Millions of the double-imaged cards were sold. These carried the imprints of such publishers and photographers as E. & H. T. Anthony, Carleton E. Watkins, Eadweard J. Muybridge, William Henry Jackson, Kilburn Brothers, and, in later years, Underwood & Underwood and the Keystone View Company.

The three-dimensional views brought new worlds into the parlor—European cathedrals, the Western frontier, Civil War battlefields. They offered tours of great cities, revealed the pyramids of Egypt, and explored the ruins of ancient Greece. Seen through the stereoscope, the already exotic images unfolded in depth, an effect that must have fired countless thousands of imaginations.

The stereo views were so widespread that many people's first glimpses of such wonders as Niagara Falls or the Grand Canyon were through the stereoscope. William Henry Jackson's views of the Yellowstone were distributed in Congress in 1871, and his awesome stereo vistas certainly influenced the vote that established our first National Park.

Photographers worked closer to home as well. Some of the finest nineteenth-century stereographs, from a historical viewpoint, are those commissioned from local cameramen. For a fee a farmer could have a view taken of his family in front of the house, or a shopkeeper could have a stereo portrait made of his workers outside the store. Because these images are less refined than the published views, and because they almost always show scenes that have vanished, they are especially valuable documents of the past, preserving a wealth of detail about how people lived and worked.

OPPOSITE PAGE: A Wisconsin family poses in front of their farmhouse and barn. Photographed about 1875, by Andreas Dahl
BELOW: A Boston print and frame shop, about 1870

A French audience in 1890 watches a three-dimensional lantern-slide show, projected anaglyphically. The viewers wore red and green goggles to produce the illusion of depth. The principle at work was the same one behind the orange and blue pictures in this book.

The huge popularity of stereoscopic views from the 1850s on naturally led to investigation in other aspects of three-dimensional reproduction. In 1858 in Paris Joseph d'Almeida introduced a method of projecting three-dimensional pictures using complementary colored images and filters. By d'Almeida's method a pair of stereo images was projected as colored transparencies of opposite hues—one orange and one blue, for instance—and viewed through filters of matching colors. Through the orange filter the eye sees only the blue image, and through the blue filter, the orange image. With your red and blue glasses on, you can give yourself a practical demonstration of d'Almeida's principle, which we have used in printing the illustrations for *Amazing 3-D*. These pictures are called anaglyphs.

D'Almeida's principles were refined by Molteni and later applied to printing by Louis Duhauron of Algiers,

who obtained patents in France in 1891 (no. 216,465) and in the United States in 1895 (no. 544,666). He claimed in the American patent that the printed anaglyphs gave a much more striking effect than the projected ones, as they employed "neither darkness, screen, nor magic lantern." In the late 1890s examples of this new form of stereoscopic printing began to appear as inserts in Sunday newspapers.

The introduction of flexible photographic film in the 1880s also brought far-reaching changes to the realm of 3-D. Amateur photographers—whose ranks had included many stereoscopic cameramen—received a boost in the 1890s as companies like the Eastman Kodak Company began marketing products that made photography simpler and cheaper than it had ever been. In 1896 a French firm, Jules Richard, started selling the "Verascope"—a compact stereo camera that looked like a clumsy pair of opera glasses—and

The Stereo Brownie camera made 3-D photography simple for amateurs in 1901.

in 1901 Kodak introduced the No. 2 Stereo Kodak and the Stereo Brownie. These simple cameras brought three-dimensional picture taking within the grasp of the casual snapshooter.

Flexible film was also the key to the practical development of motion pictures, and it was not long before experimenters were toying with stereoscopic movies. Records of early tests and trials are virtually nonexistent, but public screenings generally drew the attention of local newspapers. The first 3-D film on record premiered on June 10, 1915, at the Astor Theater in New York. The work of filmmakers Edwin S. Porter and William E. Waddell, the anaglyphic program showed random scenes of New York and New Jersey.

From that inauspicious beginning, three-dimensional film was launched on its fitful career. Three more ventures into 3-D appeared in 1922, including the world's first 3-D feature, *The Power of Love.* Filmmaker/inventor Harry K. Fairall produced this groundbreaker in anaglyph form. It opened at the Ambassador Hotel Theater in Los Angeles on September 27, 1922, to favorable reviews.

Over the Christmas holidays that year William Van Doren Kelley showed his "Plasticon" anaglyphic short, *Movies of the Future,* at New York's Rivoli Theater and followed it up early in 1923 with a "Plasticon" travelog on Washington, D.C.

Competing with the Rivoli show was a demonstration at the Selwyn Theater of the "Teleview" three-dimensional system developed by Laurens Hammond and William F. Cassidy. In a radical and expensive departure from anaglyphic 3-D, the Teleview system projected rapidly alternating black-and-white images on the screen from two interlocked projectors. Rotating shutter devices mounted in front of each seat in the theater, and synchronized to the projectors, mechanically blocked the view of first the left then the right

An audience watches a Teleview 3-D presentation at New York's Selwyn Theater in 1922. The theater seats were equipped with motor-driven viewing devices, synchronized with the projector, that alternately blocked the left and right eyes.

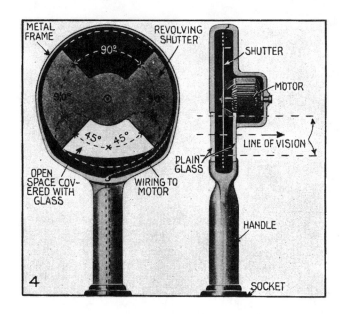

An advertisement for the world premiere of the Teleview system, December 27, 1922. Reviewers wrote of being "startled and delighted" by the "unusual effects." ABOVE RIGHT: The Teleview viewers contained a thin aluminum shutter that rotated at high speed in time with the projector to separate the two images projected on the screen. RIGHT: A 1923 advertisement for *Plastigrams*, an anaglyphic 3-D short produced by Frederick Eugene Ives and Jacob Leventhal.

eyes of the viewers. The Selwyn Theater program included a stereoscopic shadow dance performed by live actors, scenic slides, a short film on Hopi and Navajo Indians, and a feature presenting a trip to Mars. Reviews of the program—especially the feature—as well as the impracticality of installing the specialized equipment in theaters, led to the demise of Teleview.

3-D production continued in 1923 at the Fort Lee, New Jersey, studio of Frederick Eugene Ives and Jacob Leventhal. Their first film, an anaglyphic short called *Plastigrams*, was released late that year by Educational Pictures.

Pathé released four more films by Ives and Leventhal—*A Runaway Taxi*, *Ouch*, *Zowie*, and *Lunacy*, at eight-week intervals in 1925, under the series title *Stereoscopics*.

The world missed a chance to see 3-D film turned

to serious artistic purposes in Able Gance's 1925 tour-de-force, *Napoleon*. Portions of the film were shot in a three-camera panoramic combination—the forerunner of the Cinerama three-strip process—and portions in anaglyphic stereo. As Gance recalled the 3-D footage, "To see the rushes, I had to wear those red and green spectacles. The 3-D effects were very good, and very pronounced. I remember one scene where soldiers were waving their pistols in the air with excitement, and the pistols seemed to come right out into the audience." Unfortunately, the 3-D segments were edited out of the final version of the film.

After this burst of activity, stereoscopic movies slipped into one of their recurring periods of obscurity. The 3-D process did not drop out of sight, however. The Keystone View Company continued to make and sell views for the stereoscope, sending photographers around the world to keep their stock up to date. And

a new Chicago publisher, the MacyArt Process Corporation, began publishing books of anaglyphic views and promoting anaglyph printing through American Colortype, a Chicago printer.

Alfred Macy, of MacyArt, was granted a patent in 1921 for improvements on the anaglyph process, including a method of making objects in the picture project toward the viewer at calculated distances. Throughout the 1920s the company published books of stereo views printed anaglyphically, and, on the dubious strength of their patent they seem also to have licensed others to print with anaglyphs through American Colortype, their "sole producer." Though some clients may have unwittingly paid extra for a process that was available free, anaglyphic printing had found a new spokesman, and for many years American Colortype worked to interest advertisers and publishers in the system. In the 1920s and 1930s the printer prepared special 3-D advertising brochures for such products as Erector sets and Mohawk rubber tires.

A father shows his son how to use the Erector set. From a promotional brochure printed by American Colortype, about 1930

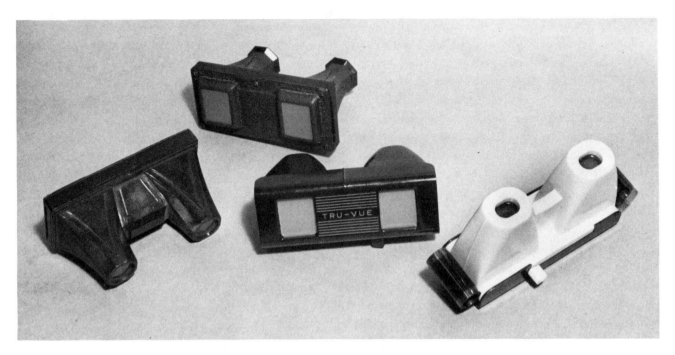

Various Tru-Vue viewers. The two at the left are from the 1930s; the two at the right from the 1940s.

In 1933 the Tru-Vue Company of Rock Island, Illinois, introduced a new format for stereoscopic views: the 35-mm filmstrip. The company launched its first series of stereoscopic filmstrips at the nearby Century of Progress Exposition in Chicago that summer, and, whether by design or accident, breathed new life into the market for 3-D. By 1933 the Keystone View Company—the last publisher of the old-style stereoscopic views—had found its business on shaky ground. Because of the depressed economy they were forced to cut back on the quality of the materials they used. They were able to rebound the next year, but only briefly. The stereoscope had become an old-fashioned contraption, and the public was ready for new ideas. Keystone published its last views in 1939.

Tru-Vue filled in brightly where the old stereoscope

Tru-Vue filmstrips and boxes. The earliest box is the second from the left; the latest is on the far right. The tightly wound strips hold their coil so well that they can spring across the room if not carefully handled.

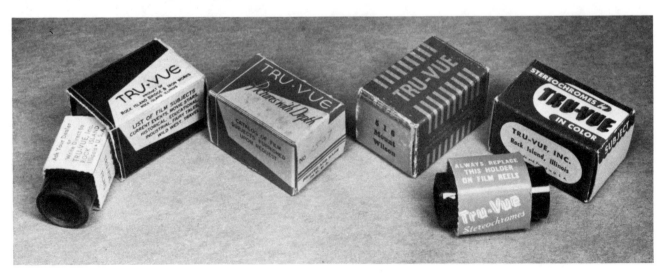

had begun to fade. The filmstrips were cheap to produce and easy to store—they coiled tightly to fit a tiny box—and the Tru-Vue viewer looked distinctly modern. The company certainly chose a progressive setting—the Century of Progress Exposition—for its first big sales push and for one of its first series of views.

Tru-Vue prospered throughout the 1930s and 1940s. They quickly expanded their list to include four hundred strips and kept it current with constant updating and replacement. By 1949 the company reported sales of 1.5 million filmstrips a year.

The filmstrips, in their little colored boxes, can occasionally be found at flea markets and garage sales for reasonable prices. The earliest boxes, from the 1930s, are printed in red and white or blue and white, with the title stamped on the top. Red-and-silver- or red-and-white-striped boxes were used through the

1940s, and color strips were produced between 1950 and 1952 in red, yellow, and blue boxes. Each filmstrip contains fourteen views printed on a brown-base film. And each strip carries the date of its production, in tiny roman numerals on the first or last frame. Because Tru-Vue selected fourteen views for each subject—and some rated a series of strips; eight for the Century of Progress Exposition—many of the images look looser and less carefully made than their counterparts on single stereoscopic cards. People walking by concessions at the Century of Progress Exposition are frozen in "off" moments along with trash cans and litter, in shots that might have been edited out had the strips been made with fewer pictures. As a result, though, the filmstrips offer a more honest look at the scenes and events of the period. They give the modern viewer the feeling of really being there.

The Infant Incubator display at the Century of Progress Exposition, Chicago, 1933. From one of the earliest Tru-Vue filmstrips

Cover of the Tru-Vue film list, about 1940

An almost unbelievable achievement of science - Premature babies "hatched" to health and happiness

SEE THE WORLD!

thru

TRU-VUE

positively life-like...

Third Dimension Pictures ★ Still Movies With Depth

Enroute in the forty-four passenger air
liner which provides every comfort.

During their years of glory the filmstrips were used to document the insides of factories, the great ocean liners, major construction projects such as the carving of Mt. Rushmore, as well as the activities of such personalities as Sally Rand and Gypsy Rose Lee. Tru-Vue served as a faithful reporter of its era, and, as the years go by, the little strips will certainly grow in historical value.

Views from early Tru-Vue films. OPPOSITE PAGE: Interior of a 1934 passenger airplane, from "Air Voyage to Jamaica." RIGHT: Gypsy Rose Lee, in "The Difference Between a Tease and a Striptease." BELOW: Sally Rand performs her famous Bubble Dance, which, according to the text on the filmstrip, was "hailed as the most important and sensational event of the Century of Progress Exposition."

"Oh, Boys . . . If I take THAT off, I'll catch cold."

The dream rest lightly in the cool, calm brilliance of mad moonlight.

Resting gently . . a vision of silvery lovliness . . embracing her dream bubble of beauty.

The other major 3-D development in the mid-1930s came from the Cambridge, Massachusetts, laboratory of Edwin H. Land. In 1932, while still an undergraduate at Harvard, Land developed a light-polarizing material that could be manufactured economically. The principle of polarizing filters had long been understood, but Land was the first to find a way to make a polarizing material in quantity. Basically, the filter acts as a comb that allows light to pass through only if its waves are oriented in the same direction as the lines in the filter. Two filters placed across each other at right angles effectively block out all light.

Land hoped to sell the material to the automobile industry for reducing headlight glare in night driving. He also began quietly experimenting with applying the polarizing material to three-dimensional photography, as did many others around the world. Polarizing filters could be made to do what anaglyph filters had done before—block out one of two images projected on a screen—with the added advantage that they caused no color distortion. Polarized light at last allowed the projection of full-color three-dimensional film.

In January 1936 Land and two associates, George W. Wheelwright III and Clarence Kennedy, gave a public demonstration, at the Waldorf Astoria Hotel in New York, of their early work with three-dimensional projection. They showed both stills and movies in black and white and in full color. This was less than a year after Kodachrome had been introduced as 16-mm movie film and months before it was made available for still cameras. The public responded enthusiastically to the double novelty of good color photography and clear three-dimensional projection.

A polarized three-dimensional movie was installed later in 1936 at the New York Museum of Science and Industry, where it played to capacity audiences for months, held over well beyond its scheduled five-week run. In Italy that same year the first polarized 3-D feature, *Nozze Vagabond* (*Beggar's Wedding*), appeared, and a year later Germany released its first color 3-D feature, *Zum Greifen Nah* (*You Can Nearly Touch It*).

In this country, impetus for commercial exploitation of three-dimensional film next came from the 1939 New York World's Fair. The Chrysler Motors Corporation commissioned John Norling and Polaroid to make a fifteen-minute film to play as the main attraction of the Chrysler exhibit. Norling had worked with Jacob Leventhal—of *Plastigrams* fame—to produce a pair of anaglyphic shorts, which had been packaged by Pete Smith and released by MGM in 1936 and 1938 under the titles *Audioscopiks* and *New Audioscopiks*.

A 1938 advertisement for Pete Smith's *New Audioscopiks*

M·G·M's *New* AUDIOSCOPIKS
EXPLANATORY REMARKS BY PETE SMITH

Screen it fast! Advertise it Big! Showmen cleaned up with the first one. The NEW AUDIOSCOPIKS is unquestionably the greatest gross-building Short Subject ever made!

With brilliant technical assistance from Polaroid, and with an ample budget from Chrysler, Norling easily surpassed his earlier achievements. In its first year, the Chrysler film was seen by 1.5 million people. Remade in color for the second year of the fair, it continued to draw crowds. Polaroid made two different styles of viewing spectacles for the film, which certainly rank among the finest 3-D glasses ever made. Both were printed and cut to look like an oncoming car, with the headlights as the filters. The audiences, wearing these miniature grilles over their eyes while dodging hurtling crankshafts and speeding Plymouths from the film, must have presented one of the wildest sights at the fair.

World War II put a damper on 3-D filmmaking for several years. In Moscow, a theater was built specifically to show lenticular 3-D films. A lensed screen allowed viewers in certain areas of the theater to see films in depth without glasses, and two new films were shown there in 1941. That same year MGM released a last Pete Smith short, *Third Dimension Murder*. But these were the last commercial 3-D films to see the light of a projector until after the war.

Three-dimensional filmmaking was submerged again in its recurring life and death drama, but happily other aspects of the 3-D field were ready and waiting to fill the gap.

ABOVE: Pete Smith with one of the actors on the set of *Third Dimension Murder*. BELOW: Polarizing glasses from the film *In Tune with Tomorrow*, shown in the Chrysler Motors theater at the 1939 New York World's Fair

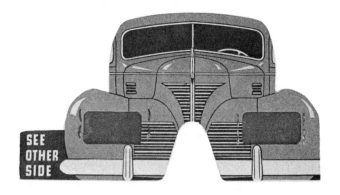

2.

REELS TO REALISTS

Stereo Photography Comes of Age

Nineteen thirty-nine was a year crowded with momentous events for 3-D and the world. In Hollywood it was the year of *The Wizard of Oz* and *Gone with the Wind*; in book publishing *The Grapes of Wrath* appeared. It was the year the atom was first split in a laboratory and the year Germany invaded Poland.

Oblivious to the dark clouds on the horizon, the 1939 New York World's Fair, whose theme was "Building the World of Tomorrow," opened its futuristic doors. Tru-Vue filmstrips document visitors streaming around the fair's many dazzling structures and walking up the Helicline into the theme buildings, the Trylon and the Perisphere. In the dome of the Perisphere audiences watched an eleven-strip panoramic film that

covered the inside walls; it was the work of Fred Waller, who would later refine his process into three-strip Cinerama. Every day in the Chrysler exhibit thousands held their car-shaped glasses to their eyes to watch their first polarized three-dimensional film—while Edwin Land demonstrated a truly new 3-D image, the Vectograph, at a nearby convention. And in gift shops all over the fairgrounds, the public found a new 3-D souvenir to bring home—the View-Master.

Everyone who grew up after 1945 remembers the View-Master, with its disks of little colored pictures, and most will fondly recall a particularly cherished reel—such as *Bambi*, *The Christmas Story*, or *Rin Tin Tin*. The first reels, produced in 1939, presented scenic views, and, since Sawyer's, the manufacturer, was based in Portland, Oregon, the emphasis was on the American West.

OPPOSITE PAGE: A View-Master scene of the 1939 New York World's Fair. BELOW: An early View-Master advertisement. RIGHT: The first View-Master model, showing hinged back, and an early viewing reel

Sawyer's had come to making View-Masters largely by accident. The firm was founded in 1914 by Carleton Sawyer and two associates as a photo-finishing service for the Owl Drug Company of Portland. In 1919 the still-tiny business was purchased by a group of investors who expanded its service to drugstores throughout the Pacific Northwest and who then shifted it into the production of scenic postcards. A chance meeting in 1938 brought together Harold Graves, then president of Sawyer's, and William Gruber, the inventor of the View-Master system.

Gruber had grown up in Germany and had been interested in stereo photography from the age of fifteen. After moving to the United States as a young man, he found work building pianos and organs, but kept up his photography as a hobby. He enjoyed tinkering with cameras and pieced together stereo models of his own design from available flat cameras. In 1938 he devised the View-Master system as an inexpensive way of making full-color stereo views using the new Kodachrome film. As he imagined it, the disk system would combine several features: pictures half the width of standard 35-mm film—and therefore half as expensive to make as full-width images—a circular card holding a series of stereo views, and a simple, sturdy viewer with an advance lever that made it easy to switch from view to view.

Gruber and his new wife, Norma, made a trip to the Oregon Caves in 1938, and Gruber brought along a stereo camera he had built from two Bantam Spe-

The exit tunnel at the Oregon Caves, from one of the first View-Master reels

cials (a popular Kodak camera). Norma made a wish on a wishing stone there that something good would come of her husband's disk idea. As she remembers it, when they came out of the cave, "Harold Graves noticed his camera while we were watching deer, and they began talking." It was there, at the Oregon Caves, that the View-Master began to grow from idea into reality.

Sawyer's moved quickly. Before the end of 1938 they were in production with their first viewer and a number of reels. The first model viewer, made of black

View-Master viewers. Clockwise from bottom center: first model, introduced in 1938; second model, introduced in 1944; square model, introduced in 1946; Model E, introduced in 1956; Model D, or "focussing viewer," introduced in 1955

plastic and metal, had a hinged back, which opened to allow easy reel change. The hole in the center of the reel fit over a spindle in the viewer in the manner of a record player. Though in modern viewers the reels are loaded through a top slot, they are still made with the center hole to fit the earliest viewers. A second model, also with a hinged back, but with streamlined styling, replaced the first version in 1944, and was replaced in turn in 1946 by a square top-loading model. The two earliest models, which originally sold for $1.50 each, now fetch prices of up to thirty dollars.

During the war Sawyer's ran at capacity production level to supply the Army and Navy with viewers and training reels. They also slowly but steadily added to their list of commercial reels in order to be ready to expand their civilian sales when demand from the military stopped.

In 1946 Sawyer's released the first of their fairy-tale reels, which featured scenes created by Florence Thompson from plaster, paint, and bits of wood, paper, and dried flowers. Included in the first series were *Little Red Riding Hood*, *Hansel and Gretel*, and *Snow White*. Later the line grew to include *Little Black Sambo*, *Aladdin and the Wonderful Lamp*, *Sam Sawyer*, and *20,000 Leagues Under the Sea*.

Also, in the years just after the war, the company expanded the range of its list to encompass scenic views of England, Switzerland, the West Indies, and the Middle East. They published two books with View-Master reels as illustrations: *Succulent Plants* and *Alpine Wild Flowers of the Western United States*. And they added a popular series of Bible stories staged with live actors.

By combining low cost—35¢ for the reels, $1.50 or $2.00 for the viewers—with full color in a simple and attractive system, Sawyer's was able to revive interest in stereo views and bring them back as a common household fixture. Sales of View-Master reels and viewers skyrocketed every year through the 1940s and continued to grow through the 1950s, as new products and views were released.

TOP: Plastic-molding machines at Sawyer's Progress, Oregon, plant in 1954. The machines operated around the clock making the bodies for Tru-View and View-Master viewers. CENTER: Florence Thomas, creator of the fairy-tale scenes, stands among some of her works in a 1954 photograph. BOTTOM: View-Master promotional displays made the reels stand out in stores.

View-Master views from the late 1940s and early 1950s. OPPOSITE PAGE, clockwise from top left: the Grand Canyon; Times Square at night; inside Boulder Dam; a scene from *Little Black Sambo*; the genie from *Aladdin and the Wonderful Lamp*; a field of California wildflowers. ABOVE: Maori men perform the Haka war dance. BELOW LEFT: Gretel pushes the witch into the oven in a scene from *Hansel and Gretel*. BELOW RIGHT: Tarzan bellows; Cheta sings along.

Another company that did big business in stereo during the war was Polaroid, whose Vectograph three-dimensional images were used extensively in training manuals and in aerial surveillance. The Vectograph, which Land first demonstrated to the Optical Society of America in late 1939, was a fundamentally new kind of image, made to be seen through polarizing filters.

After their success with three-dimensional projection in 1935, Land and his associates began to investigate ways of making 3-D prints using polarized light. The problem they faced was how to overlay two images, with cross-angled polarizers, in such a way that the polarizers did not combine to block out the entire picture. The solution was to abandon the filters as they were used in projection and to make the image itself a light polarizer. Thus the Vectograph is not an ordinary picture. It is not made of pigments, dyes, or photographic silver grains, but instead renders its image by degree of polarization.

The darkest areas in the Vectograph are made of a perfect light polarizer—seen as black through a filter of cross-grained polarization—the middle tones are made of various degrees of imperfect polarizer, and the white areas have no polarizer at all. By the nature of the polarizing material, such an image will be invisible when looked at through a polarizing filter if the optical grains of filter and image are parallel. But if the two are crossed at right angles, the image will be clearly formed. And, because the polarizer exists only within the image, two such pictures, made from optical grains at crossed angles, can be overlayed for stereo viewing.

Land published a full description of the process in the June 1940 issue of the *Journal of the Optical Society of America*. He ended the article with the news that full-color Vectographs had already been made in Polaroid's laboratory.

Almost immediately work turned to adapting the process for military use. Processing kits were made to fit in portable cases, and Polaroid quickly set up a military training center in a Cambridge warehouse— even before the United States entered the war.

Vectographs were used extensively in the early years of the war as three-dimensional illustrations in military instruction manuals. The prints could be bound into a book to show the workings of intricate machinery or to illustrate how a rifle came apart for cleaning. The other major use of Vectographs was for stereo aerial photography. As prints of any size could be easily viewed with a simple pair of glasses, and as

The Vectograph, developed by Polaroid, combined left and right stereo images on a single piece of film to be viewed through cross-polarized glasses. One of the most ingenious and sophisticated methods of making stereo images, the Vectograph also proved to be an ideal medium for three-dimensional aerial photography. RIGHT: A Polaroid classroom in Cambridge, Massachusetts, where military personnel learned to make Vectographs during World War II

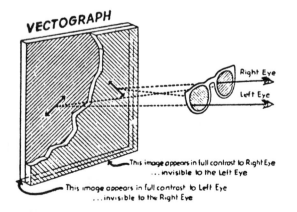

VECTOGRAPH

Right Eye

Left Eye

This image appears in full contrast to Right Eye
...invisible to the Left Eye

This image appears in full contrast to Left Eye
...invisible to the Right Eye

several prints could be patched together to show a large area of land, Vectographs proved the ideal medium for aerial reconnaissance photography. They were carried along on bombing missions, used to study enemy troop movements, and—at the height of their tour of duty—called on to create a 3-D image of the coast of France for the Allied invasion at Normandy.

After the war Polaroid promoted Vectographs as advertising and marketing aids—for use in such things as sample books and window displays. But, because they had to be prepared individually and by hand, they were simply too expensive for widespread use. Instead of lingering over a stubborn problem, and investing time and money in new methods of production, Polaroid set off in quest of instant photography, using some of the image-transfer technology developed for the Vectograph. By early 1947 the unstoppable Polaroid researchers had developed a system for making instant prints, and the following year the company began selling the first Polaroid Land cameras.

Vectographs nearly returned in 1954, when Polaroid and Technicolor agreed to collaborate on the production and processing of full-color Vectographic movie film, but the project fizzled when the demand for 3-D movies disappeared. You can still have Vectographs custom made from your own stereo negatives by the Stereo Optical Company, 3539 North Kenton Avenue, Chicago, Illinois 60641. The price for a single 5 × 7-inch print is about two hundred dollars, but the company also sells materials and instructions for doing it yourself.

Vectograph diagram from a navigation manual

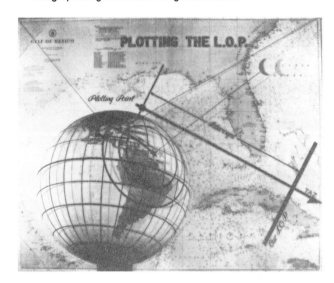

NOTE: The illustrations on these two pages are anaglyphic (red and blue) reproductions of original Vectographs. They show the depth, but not the quality of the originals.

A rare demonstration Vectograph made by Polaroid to show the value of the process in military reconnaissance work

The first advertisement, November 1945, for the Stereo Realist camera. The camera was not actually available in stores until late 1947.

A 1946 advertisement for the Stereo Realist camera, showing the sophisticated—and often surreal—graphics used by the David White Company

The close of World War II may have signaled the end for the Vectograph, but the following years of suburban prosperity were a time of rebirth for amateur stereo photography. In the November 1945 issue of *American Photography* magazine, a full-page advertisement from the David White Company announced the new Stereo Realist, the first of the postwar 35-mm stereo cameras.

The Stereo Realist was designed and named by Seton Rochwhite, a longtime stereo buff who became a 3-D crusader in the late 1930s while waiting impatiently for manufacturers to create a stereo camera to use the new Kodachrome color film. In 1929, when Rochwhite first became interested in stereo photography, he built himself a camera out of parts from two Kodak box cameras. A more complex 35-mm device followed in 1932, and in 1938 he designed a modern stereo camera for commercial manufacture.

His prototype, finished in 1940, took paired pictures

measuring 22 × 24 millimeters—the format that would eventually become the American standard for stereo. Rochwhite worked as a lighting engineer for the Wisconsin Electric Power Company, and his boss there, Ivan Illing, suggested he try taking his stereo camera idea to the David White Company, Milwaukee manufacturers of surveying equipment and other precision optical instruments. Rochwhite did, the firm expressed an interest in his plans, and in 1943 he began working there, redesigning his camera for mass production.

The 1945 advertisement pictured the camera and its companion slide viewer. Enticing copy described the pictures taken with it as "more *natural*, more excitingly real than any you've ever taken." Ads in the following months must have kept readers drooling. "Thrill to your own pictures in breath-taking third dimension." ". . . opens a wonderful new world of photographic experiences." ". . . all the color, depth and vibrance of real life . . ." "Wait till you get your hands on the New Stereo Realist." But it was not until the fall of 1947 that the camera finally arrived in stores, its production beset along the way by postwar shortages of parts and materials.

In the meantime, the photography magazines kept anxious would-be stereo buffs at bay with articles about old cameras such as the Heidoscope, Rolleidoscope, and Stereoflektoscope from Germany, the various models from the French manufacturer Richard, and the Swiss Kern. The magazines also bought time by discussing stereo attachments that fit over the lenses of ordinary flat cameras—the Stereoloy for Leica cameras, and the Kentucky-made Stereo-Tach for most others. But you could almost hear the sigh of relief when magazine reviewers finally got their hands on the actual Stereo Realist.

Herbert McKay began his review in *American Photography* with the words "At last," and went on to rave about the camera's "smooth, streamlined" design, free of "unsightly knobs, bumps, and blisters." The Realist is an elegant machine, and was quite modern looking in its day. Rochwhite had come to its design with an open mind, shifting the basic components to positions that made engineering sense, but that broke with manufacturing tradition. The viewfinder, for example, is on the bottom of the camera, and the shutter release on the left side.

The reviews were favorable, the ads were sensational, and the public responded by buying into stereo—at the Realistic price of $162.50. The cameras accounted for almost nine percent of David White's net sales in 1947, after only a few months in the stores. By 1952 that figure would grow to sixty-seven percent. To make stereo photography as easy as possible for the new Realist owners, David White set up a slide-mounting service. Stereo film sent to Kodak was processed and automatically forwarded to Milwaukee for mounting.

The Realist simplified and publicized stereo photography and transformed it from an old black-and-white holdover into a modern color sensation. Realist buyers came to three-dimensional photography as if it was brand new. And in many ways it was.

When people first see stereo color slides they invariably ooh and ah, and say things like, "That's fantastic. I've never seen anything like it." or "I wish I had

The Stereo-Tach fit over the lens of an ordinary camera, splitting a single frame into a pair of stereo images. The attachment was available as early as 1941, but the manufacturers did not begin to advertise heavily until 1951.

The Stereo Realist was simple to use, and, with the David White Company's mounting service, stereo slides were no more bother to have processed than ordinary flat pictures.

Simple, fast to operate! Hold camera against forehead for steadiness, focus and view subject — click the shutter and you've taken a Stereo-REALIST picture!

No special requirements in film or processing. Stereo-REALIST uses standard 35MM color film obtainable everywhere. Follow mailing instructions with film roll.

Pictures come back mounted — ready to use. Beautiful life-like color transparencies mounted in Stereo-Pairs — the secret of their depth.

Put your pictures in the self-illuminated Stereo-REALIST Viewer and WOW! You'll see your pictures life-size with true depth and full color.

3-D snapshots. Clockwise from top: a stylish Terri Tucker in Seattle; Miss New Jersey beams with pride; Jeff Burger test drives his Christmas present, a 1953 toy police car; the Morgan family poses on a Massachusetts patio (coauthor Hal Morgan at the far left).

3-D slides of *my* family." Stereo slides are as different from ordinary snapshots as meteors are from golfballs. The hype in the advertisements for the Realist was *true*. Stereo really *does* bring color slides to life, and the color slides bring more realism to 3-D than black-and-white prints ever could.

With their new Stereo Realists people began to photograph the things around them in depth. Babies, pets, the car, the grandparents—all the old snapshot subjects now came under the gaze of the twin lenses. The heyday of the backyard—the lawn furniture and barbecues—was well documented in 3-D, along with Studebakers, saddle shoes, sunsuits, felt fedoras, wood-appointed station wagons, spectator pumps, string ties, crewcuts, upsweeps, pageboys, and cherry red lipstick.

Serious photographers took on more challenging

A 1955 cocktail party. Amanda and Ellen Morgan in the foreground

subjects—close-ups of flowers, time exposures at night, exaggerated depth shots ("hyperstereo") of distant scenes, and that fifties favorite, the nude. By early 1951 the camera magazines were carrying suggestive little ads for "3-D model slides" or "beauty in 3rd dimension" for the collections of devoted amateurs.

Stereo clubs began to spring up. One of the first—and by far the best publicized—was the Hollywood Stereoscopic Society, founded in 1950 by some of the biggest names in show business. A Hollywood Stereo Realist dealer, Jerry Holscher, conceived the idea for the society and did much to organize it. The first meeting was held in September at the estate of Harold Lloyd, a huge fan of the Stereo Realist who worked hard promoting 3-D photography. Officers and directors elected that first evening included Lloyd, Dick Powell, Frank Capra, Arthur Hornblow, Jr., and Art Linkletter. Among the early Stereo Realist owners who were active in the society were Ann Sothern, Charles Roscher, Cecil B. DeMille, Joan Crawford, Edgar Bergen, and Cedric Gibbons. Irene Dunne, Compton Bennett, Corinne Calvet, and George Sidney also distinguished themselves in the society's first stereo slide contest.

The sales staff at David White picked right up on the

3-D "model" slides rode in on the coattails of the stereo photography boom.

publicity potential of the star-studded group. They offered stereo slides of the society's first meeting to dealers around the country and to other fledgling stereo clubs. They had already begun a dazzling series of advertisements featuring endorsements by movie stars, and they wanted to promote the impression that the Stereo Realist was the camera preferred by the Hollywood set. Featured in the ads were Walter Huston, Dick Powell, Frank Capra, Ann Sothern (". . . the most

James H. Calder, at right, demonstrates the Stereo Realist projector at the first meeting of the Hollywood Stereoscopic Society, September 6, 1950. Listening are, from left to right, Edgar Bergen, Art Linkletter, Sterling Holloway, and Mrs. Edgar Bergen.

Harold Lloyd taking a picture with his Stereo Realist. Lloyd was a huge fan of stereo photography. He served as the first president of the Hollywood Stereoscopic Society. Between 1948 and 1954 he took more than thirty thousand stereo slides—and he worked at promoting the hobby. As he explained to a reporter in 1951, "A David White Company salesman handed me a camera and suggested that I just walk around with it for a day. I took ninety pictures in the course of that day and have been a nothing-a-year front man for the David White Company ever since."

Art Linkletter lends a hand to a 3-D model at a 1955 meeting of the Hollywood Stereoscopic Society. Linkletter started taking stereo pictures a little later than Harold Lloyd. He too became a devotee of the hobby and served as an early president of the Hollywood Stereoscopic Society.

Bob Hope

Starring in "FANCY PANTS", a Paramount picture. Color by Technicolor.

says "I took one look at Stereo-REALIST pictures and said 'Hope that's for you'. They're terrific!"

Ann Sothern

Beautiful star of M-G-M Studios — now appearing in M-G-M's Technicolor production "NANCY GOES TO RIO"

Says: "My Stereo-REALIST is the most fascinating camera I've ever owned — it's really easy to use — and it puts into pictures what other cameras leave out — beautiful, life-like 3rd dimension."

Fred Astaire

Famous star of Paramount Pictures, co-starring in "LET'S DANCE". Color by Technicolor.

says: "My Stereo-REALIST makes me my favorite cameraman. I take pictures so real they're actually beyond belief!"

Cecil B. de Mille

Famous Producer-Director of Paramount's Technicolor "Samson and Delilah"

Says: "My Stereo-REALIST takes what I've waited a life-time to see — the perfect picture!"

Stereo Realist advertisements from 1949 and 1950. For two years the David White Company ran regular ads in such magazines as *National Geographic* and *American Photography*. These featured a dazzling array of stars giving personal endorsements of the camera. Most of the personalities seem to

have been genuine fans of 3-D. OPPOSITE PAGE: The Stereo Realist's most famous fan. This photograph was taken by David Douglas Duncan in early 1952, when General Eisenhower, then commander of NATO, visited Istanbul. It appeared as a full-page illustration in *Life* magazine in March 1952.

fascinating camera I've ever owned."), Harold Lloyd, John Wayne, Nancy Olson, Cecil B. DeMille (". . . takes what I've waited a lifetime to see—the perfect picture."). Fred Astaire, Bob Hope, Joan Crawford ("It's a favorite with me."), Virginia Mayo, Gregory Peck, Edgar Bergen, and Jane Wyman. No one could say the camera suffered from a lack of glamorous backers.

The camera's most influential endorsement came some months later when, in early 1952, General Dwight D. Eisenhower was pictured in *Life* magazine

gaily photographing with his Stereo Realist in Istanbul. Newspapers around the country ran similar photographs, and in August *Fortune* magazine printed a story about Eisenhower and his Stereo Realist, and made prominent mention of the David White Company. About five hundred of Eisenhower's stereo slides—which document his days as a general in Europe, the 1952 presidential campaign, and his White House years—are now safely stored at the Eisenhower Library in Abilene, Kansas.

A sampling of Eisenhower's 3-D snapshots.
OPPOSITE PAGE, TOP: News photographers try to
take Ike's picture as he counterattacks in 3-D.
Eisenhower is flanked in the press's picture by
Mamie and her mother. OPPOSITE PAGE, BOTTOM:
In a classic head-of-state snapshot, Eisenhower
catches Winston Churchill grinning over a
monstrous cigar while John Foster Dulles leans in
at the right. ABOVE: Eager spectators at the
inaugural parade, January 1953. Probably taken
by an aide with the President's camera. RIGHT:
Young Barbara Anne and David pay an early
morning call on their grandmother.

ABOVE: The TDC Stereo Vivid, the first projector designed for 3-D projection of Realist-format stereo slides. LEFT: A 1952 all-American family watches a 3-D home slide show with polarizing glasses and the Stereo Realist projector.

By mid-1952 the 3-D photography market was red hot. *Popular Mechanics* featured an article with the headline "Stereo Photography Sweeps the Country." The Stereo Realist was selling at a rate of forty thousand a year, and several other manufacturers had put out, or were preparing to put out, competing models.

The TDC Stereo Vivid projector, which first appeared in the spring of 1950, made it possible to project Realist-format stereo slides. Built by the Three Dimension Company of Chicago, the projector allowed stereo slides to be enjoyed by a group, and stereo clubs were soon drawing huge crowds to their slide shows.

In the summer of 1951, the Stereo Vivid was challenged by the Stereo Realist projector from the David White Company, a sleekly designed, optically deluxe machine. But at $290—compared to $165 for the Stereo Vivid—the Realist projector was only for those who demanded the best.

The David White Company began to be undersold on its camera as well. Late in 1950 the German Iloca arrived on the American market with a price tag of $125. The Iloca took wider pictures than the Realist—30 × 24 millimeters—and fewer of them per roll, and it required a special slide viewer to see the full frame

width. But it was the first real competitor to the Realist. Then the Busch Verascope F40 arrived in the spring of 1951 to steal some of the better-heeled customers away from David White. Built by the Richard company of France, the Verascope F40 had been given a special leather and chrome finish for the American market. It took the same wide pictures as the Iloca, and it cost $287—no plaything for the Sunday snapshooter.

David White countered with a deluxe-model Realist, the ST 42, and lashed out in its advertising against the foreign competition. "The Realist is more than a stereo camera—it's a 100% American-designed, American-

Three stereo cameras from 1950 and 1951. Top to bottom: the Iloca, the Busch Verascope F40, and the Videon Stereo

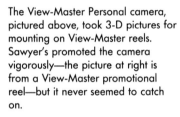

"TAKE PICTURES LIKE THIS FOR LESS COST THAN SNAPSHOTS".

The View-Master Personal camera, pictured above, took 3-D pictures for mounting on View-Master reels. Sawyer's promoted the camera vigorously—the picture at right is from a View-Master promotional reel—but it never seemed to catch on.

made, precision optical instrument," read a June 1951 ad. David White soon had to watch its home court as well. Another Milwaukee company, Videon Camera Sales, charged in with the $99.50 Videon Stereo camera in September, and Keys Stereo Products revived the tiny Haneel Tri-Vision camera—first produced in 1946—at the "grab-it" price of only $29.95.

By 1952 Sawyer's had sold six million of its two-dollar View-Master viewers and deduced that it had a ready market for its own stereo camera. In June the company brought out the View-Master Personal stereo camera, at a price of $149, for making home snapshots to fit View-Master reels.

Designed by Gordon Smith, the camera took the miniature View-Master pictures on regular 35-mm film and accomplished this without waste. A lens shift, dubbed the "Film Miser," allowed a row of pictures to be taken along the bottom of the film strip. Then, when the end of the roll was reached, the user shifted the lenses up, and took a second row of pictures along the top until the film was rewound. Ingenious. And economical. It was also a classic case of a product

beyond the reach of its true market. How many children must have seen the camera's picture on the reel lists and wished devoutly that they could buy one. But, sadly, it was aimed at their parents' pocketbooks.

The advertisements dwelled on the savings in the system. "Takes color pictures in 3 dimensions at . . . less than the cost of ordinary black and white snapshots!" In smaller type the ad explained how buyers would have to mount their own pictures on the reels, using the "semi-automatic" View-Master film cutter.

Except for the bother of mounting the slides and the slight loss of resolution because of the small size of the images, the camera was a sensational idea. A twenty-exposure roll of Kodachrome film yielded thirty-seven stereo pairs. Including film, processing, and reels, the cost of each slide was only twelve cents. And who could deny the appeal of home-made View-Master reels?

The company also livened up its regular reel offerings at about this time, ringing in a brave new View-Master era. In 1951 Sawyer's purchased Tru-Vue, and along with it got the license to produce stereo views of Walt Disney productions. Sawyer's made a passing effort to polish up Tru-Vue, changing the filmstrip format to rectangular cards, but the intent of the purchase seems to have been to strengthen the position of View-Master. After a respectable lapse of time, View-Master began to strip Tru-Vue of its prized possessions, and reels of Disneyland, the Mickey Mouse Club, and *Bambi* began to appear.

In 1951 View-Master also launched a series featuring licensed cartoon characters: Bugs Bunny, Woody Woodpecker, Andy Panda, and Chilly Willy. They began to cash in on the draw of personalities with reels of Gene Autry, Hopalong Cassidy, the Cisco Kid, the Lone Ranger, Roy Rogers, and Dale Evans. And—in the best tradition of the old stereo cards—View-Master reels began to document what they labeled "Real Life Adventures": an aircraft carrier in action, the rodeo, firefighters, performing elephants, life on a farm, and a kangaroo hunt with Australian aborigines.

In 1953, to round out their updated product line, View-Master came out with the Stereomatic 500 projector for three-dimensional projection of View-Master reels. View-Master had put on a new face to greet the the 3-D boom, and, as one of the major market forces going into it, they were to emerge strong at the other end.

A high-quality stereo movie camera for amateurs, the Bolex Stereo, was introduced in June 1952 with some flashy advertisements. The camera took split-image stereo on a single strip of 16-mm film, for projection in a normal projector fitted with a beam-splitting lens. Riding the crest of a wave that had not yet reached the Hollywood movie industry, the manufacturers let the public know that they had a chance with the Bolex Stereo to beat the big studios to 3-D. "Years from now you'll see stereo in movie theaters, but pack that waiting period with movie thrills unique to yourself and your intimate friends."

The promised years of head start turned out to be just a few months. In November 1952 Hollywood finally responded to the public hunger for 3-D that had been unsettling the photographic industry since the advent of the Stereo Realist.

By the fall of 1952 3-D had swelled to a presence

"STREAMLINED SIMPLICITY".

ABOVE: The Bolex Stereo movie camera, introduced in June 1952, took 3-D movies on regular 16-mm film. It put amateurs a step ahead of the movie industry. LEFT: A contented family gathered in their living room for a View-Master slide show. Dad prepares the Stereomatic 500 projector. In a moment they'll dim the lights and put on their polarizing glasses.

We Left Winter Back Home for Sunny
San Antonio

the movie industry could no longer ignore. There were six different stereo cameras on the market, two projectors, at least seven different viewers, a stereo attachment for Polaroid Land cameras, and even a stereo wedding album from Holson. Realist cameras kept showing up unexpectedly in travel ads, not to mention around the necks of movie stars and Presidential candidates. And stereo slides were being used extensively in advertising and sales.

Companies like Puritan Fabrics and Columbia Lace were using stereo slides in counter displays. A Southern beekeeper sent stereo close-ups of his fancy queen

bees to prospective customers. Salesmen for Lever Brothers, National Dairy, and Schenley carried stereo slides as part of their sales kits, and the David White Company claimed that more than forty percent of the nation's casket manufacturers were using the Realist viewer to sell their wares. Even Forest Lawn Cemetery got into the act; they prepared a complete set of stereo slides illustrating their services.

The Hollywood 3-D movies, when they finally did arrive in late 1952, focused even more attention on stereo photography. And at about the same time, stereo's most influential fan, General Eisenhower, won the presidential election, bringing a Stereo Realist to the White House.

In 1953 several new 3-D cameras appeared: the Revere 33 ($174.50), the Videon II ($99.50), the Coronet ($14.95, with viewer), and the Winpro ($39.95, with viewer), as well as two projectors, the View-Master Stereomatic 500, and the Compco Triad. 1953 was also the year that the giant of the photographic industry—Eastman Kodak—awoke to 3-D. In the spring Kodak started to sell special stereo-length rolls of Kodachrome and to offer a stereo-mounting service. The price of the new K335 film roll included processing and mounting.

A sampling of stereo slide viewers from the early 1950s: 1. Linex 2. Guild 3-D 3. Stereo-Tach 4. Arcadia 5. Radex Gem 6. Kirk 7. Iloca 8. Wollensak 11 9. Realist ST-61 10. TDC

The 1952 atomic bomb test at Yucca Flats, Nevada. TOP: Mannequins in a sample ninety-dollar bomb shelter beneath the "Typical American Home." The shelter was built by the Army eleven thousand feet from ground zero. CENTER: Test cars, with mannequin drivers, set out at varying distances from the bomb site. BOTTOM: An Army "Rad-Safe" officer measures the ground with a Geiger counter.

Jayne Mansfield at Romanoff's Restaurant, Beverly Hills, about 1953. Photographed by Tommy Thomas at a meeting of the Hollywood Stereoscopic Society.

Demonstration for Estes Kefauver at the 1952 Democratic National Convention in Chicago. The 1952 party conventions were the first to be thoroughly covered on national television. Home viewers watched the workings of party politics for the first time as Eisenhower swept the Republican nomination and a hesitant Adlai Stevenson won the vote from the Democrats.

Senator Kefauver speaks on a doorstep in Chilton, Wisconsin, during the 1952 presidential campaign.

An audience in Harlem listens to a speech by President Truman in October 1952, just two weeks before Eisenhower's landslide at the polls.

1954 proved to be a watershed year for stereo photography. Eight new cameras were introduced, and for the first time sales started to slip for some. Revere and David White brought out deluxe models—the Wollensak Stereo 10 and the Super Realist—to liven up the top end of the market, and Lionel—the train people—jolted the lower end with the Linex, a miniature device that sold with a viewer, pouch, and a roll of 16-mm film for only $44.50. Two veteran stereo designers made comebacks with new cameras—Seton Rochwhite (Stereo Realist) with the Milwaukee-made Kin-Dar, and Gordon Smith (View-Master Personal) with the TDC Stereo Vivid camera. The Three Dimension Company, by this time a division of Bell & Howell, also produced the trimmed-down TDC Stereo Colorist to accompany the Stereo Vivid. From Germany came the Edixa, designed to take Realist-format slides. And at the very end of the year came the long-awaited Kodak Stereo camera.

Kodak began to pique curiosity in the stereo world in the summer with big advertisements for their stereo slide-mounting service and with the introduction of two models of Kodaslide Stereo viewers. But the Kodak Stereo camera came along like a freight train through a chicken coop. Huge advertisements and promotional fanfare announced its arrival, and the photography magazines gave it featured reviews—raves.

At $84.50, the Kodak Stereo was the cheapest stereo camera of reasonable quality, and it featured a host of technical attractions. The most imaginative was the position of the viewfinder directly between the two lenses, an arrangement made possible by mirrors. To prevent tilting and misalignment of the stereo images, a level was clearly visible through the viewer. All the controls—focus, aperture, and shutter speed—could be seen at a glance and conveniently set from the top of the camera. And the Kodak was the easiest stereo camera to load. It was, in short, the answer for stereo beginners.

The low price and the ease of operation of the Kodak Stereo camera, coupled with public faith in the Kodak name, sent the camera thundering ahead of its competitors at a time when the stereo market was already beginning to narrow. The Kin-Dar, Edixa, and Videon cameras soon disappeared, and Sawyer's ended production of the View-Master Personal in 1955, first slashing its price from the original $139.50

The 1954 stereo camera crop. From top to bottom: The Wollensak Stereo 10, perhaps the finest of the deluxe-model stereo cameras; the TDC Stereo Vivid and the TDC Stereo Colorist; the Edixa; the Kodak Stereo camera

General Eisenhower making an impromptu speech upon arrival at LaGuardia Field, New York City, in June 1952.

The B-36 atomic bomber, as seen from under the tail. This photograph was taken at Mitchell Field, New York, on May 16, 1954, Armed Forces Day.

to $89.50. The David White Company anxiously offered free weekend trials of the Stereo Realist, and, with continued advertising, managed to hang onto a healthy share of the market.

Actually, the Kodak Stereo arrived in the stores in time to dominate only the downslide of the stereo boom. A few more cameras made ill-fated debuts over the next few years—among them the Steré-all, Simda, Sputnik, Owla, Belplasca, Delta, Contura, Stereo Graphic, Realist 45, Windsor, Stereo Mikroma, and Stereo Hit—but by 1960 the public romance with stereo photography was over. Only the Stereo Realist continued in production throughout the 1960s. When production ceased in 1971, one hundred and thirty thousand cameras had been made, making the Realist the all-time stereo best seller.

All the 35-mm stereo cameras are still actively sold on the second-hand market. In good condition they are worth more today than they were when new. Kodak had abandoned its mounting service to David White in 1955, but, with the demise of the Stereo Realist, has resumed it. And the stereo processing business at Kodak has been growing steadily in recent years.

During its spotlight performance—from about 1950 through 1955—stereo was the hottest area of photography. The battery of stereo cameras that crowded the market in those years left behind a marvelous 3-D record of the era—the events and personalities, the clothes and the customs of the times. For those who were lucky enough to have stereo in the family, the little paired slides remain the best snapshots the world has ever seen.

The Revere 33 camera and Stereo 22 viewer

3.

HOLLYWOOD TAKES THE PLUNGE

The Movies Go 3-D

On Thanksgiving evening, 1952, klieg lights raked the skies over Los Angeles to announce the premiere of the film *Bwana Devil*, while inside two Paramount theaters capacity crowds wearing polarized glasses shrieked and ducked to avoid a hail of spears and an attack of man-eating lions. 3-D had arrived in Hollywood.

The next day newspapers across the country ran a brief UP report about the lion that "leaped from a screen" bringing "screams from an audience" during the first public showing of a new three-dimensional film made by a process called Natural Vision. Unfortunately, while the film's producer-director-writer, Arch Oboler, began boasting of box-office records, Los Angeles film critics resoundingly panned the movie, an unexceptional and cheaply made story of railroad construction in British East Africa.

By the end of its first week, *Bwana Devil* was an obvious commercial success. It had brought in more than $95,000 at two theaters, and an eager public formed record lines for admission.

The film industry, reeling from the competition from television, which had gone commercial in 1948, desperately needed a new way to lure the crowds away from their living rooms and back into the theaters. Thousands of movie houses had already closed—in 1952 attendance had dropped to two-thirds of its

1946 level—and the studios had cut back drastically on production. Activity was down by a half at MGM, and by two-thirds at Twentieth Century-Fox, and contract lists—those actors the studios reserved for regular business—had been slashed from nine hundred names in 1950 to just over three hundred at the end of 1952.

Many of the biggest stars—including Clark Gable, Lana Turner, and Errol Flynn—had fled to Europe to take advantage of a tax loophole available to those who spent seventeen out of eighteen months abroad. Rosalind Russell and Bette Davis retreated to the stage; Van Johnson and Betty Hutton returned to vaudeville; and many others, including George Raft, Lucille Ball, and Eve Arden, defected to television.

Hollywood was mired in depression, and groping anxiously for a means to combat its arch rival, television. Two solutions caught the public's eye—and the studios' attention—during the fall of 1952.

The first was Cinerama, the creation of Fred Waller. Projected onto a huge, wide, curved screen by three projectors, Cinerama wrapped the movie around the audience to make a film *seem* three-dimensional by involving the viewer's peripheral vision. Six separate soundtracks, played from speakers surrounding the theater, provided an added illusion of depth.

Waller's invention had been a long time in the making. He had made the eleven-strip film that was projected in patches around the inside of the Perisphere at the 1939 New York World's Fair, and for the next thirteen years he had worked to refine the system, backed along the way by Laurance Rockefeller, Time

A 1952 poster for *Bwana Devil*, the adventure film that kicked off the 3-D movie boom

53

Cinerama used a wide, curved screen and a six-track sound system to give the *impression* of three dimensions, but not true 3-D.

Inc., Hazard Reeves, and Lowell Thomas. The first commercial production, *This Is Cinerama,* was directed by Robert Flaherty, the classic documentary filmmaker and one of the cinema's most distinguished figures.

Occasional press previews were held during 1951 and 1952 in a converted Long Island tennis court in order to pique the interest of the media and the public. And both were ready when the film finally opened at New York's Broadway Theater in September 1952. The star-studded audience at the world premiere sat back in their seats and were almost immediately plunged into a roller-coaster ride that had them yelling and clutching their armrests. After a brief intermission they were flown over Niagara Falls, paddled down the canals of Venice, serenaded by the Vienna Boys' Choir, and elevated for a hawk's-eye view of the Grand Canyon.

The press went wild. In a front-page story, the *New York Times* proclaimed the audience "as excited and thrilled by the spectacle presented as if they were seeing motion pictures for the first time."

Film industry executives took note of this reaction and reviewed what they knew to be Cinerama's problems. Foremost among the drawbacks was the cost of showing the films. To project Cinerama, a theater had to install one of the specially curved screens along with entirely new projection equipment. The cost of such a conversion in a medium-size theater was estimated at $70,000 in 1952—quite a sum of money for the average theater owner. And once converted, the theater would only be equipped to show Cinerama

films, of which there was so far just one. So the studio heads decided to hold off on Cinerama—to wait and see what happened.

They didn't have long to wait. A second solution to Hollywood's problems came along just eight weeks later in the form of *Bwana Devil* and stereoscopic 3-D.

Though 3-D films were by no means new to Hollywood—Pete Smith's *Audioscopiks* had been quite popular in the 1930s—they had been missing in action since the start of World War II. The European success of the Dutch short *Queen Juliana* in 1948, and of the Spottiswood brothers' shorts for the 1951 Festival of Britain received little attention from the American film industry. It took an independent producer, Arch Oboler, to get the 3-D wheels rolling again.

Oboler had just completed *Five*—the first film to deal with the survivors of a nuclear war—when he saw a test of the Natural Vision 3-D system, a two-camera filming rig and projection system put together by Milton and Julian Gunzberg with the camera expertise of O. S. Brhyn, Friend Baker, and Lothrop Worth. The system had been seen and rejected by every major studio, but Oboler responded with instant enthusiasm.

A quick deal was struck, and filming began on *The Lions of Zulu*—retitled *Bwana Devil* before release—on June 18, 1952. The film was based on a story Oboler had heard in the late forties while on safari, of a pair of marauding lions that made meals of workers building a trans-African railroad. As star and starlet Oboler cast Robert Stack and Barbara Britton, with Nigel Bruce thrown in for support.

Despite heavy-handed advertising copy—"A lion in your lap, a lover in your arms"—the use of blatant 3-D effects was kept to a minimum. A tossed spear that was difficult to see (too small and too fast-moving), other spears poked at the cameras (too far away), a snake hanging from a tree (too close to the cameras—eyestrain!), and an occasional encounter with a pair of scrawny lions (not at all menacing), offered but a handful of simple harrassments for the audience. By far the best 3-D effect was a shot toward the end of

A full house takes in the spectacle of *Bwana Devil.*

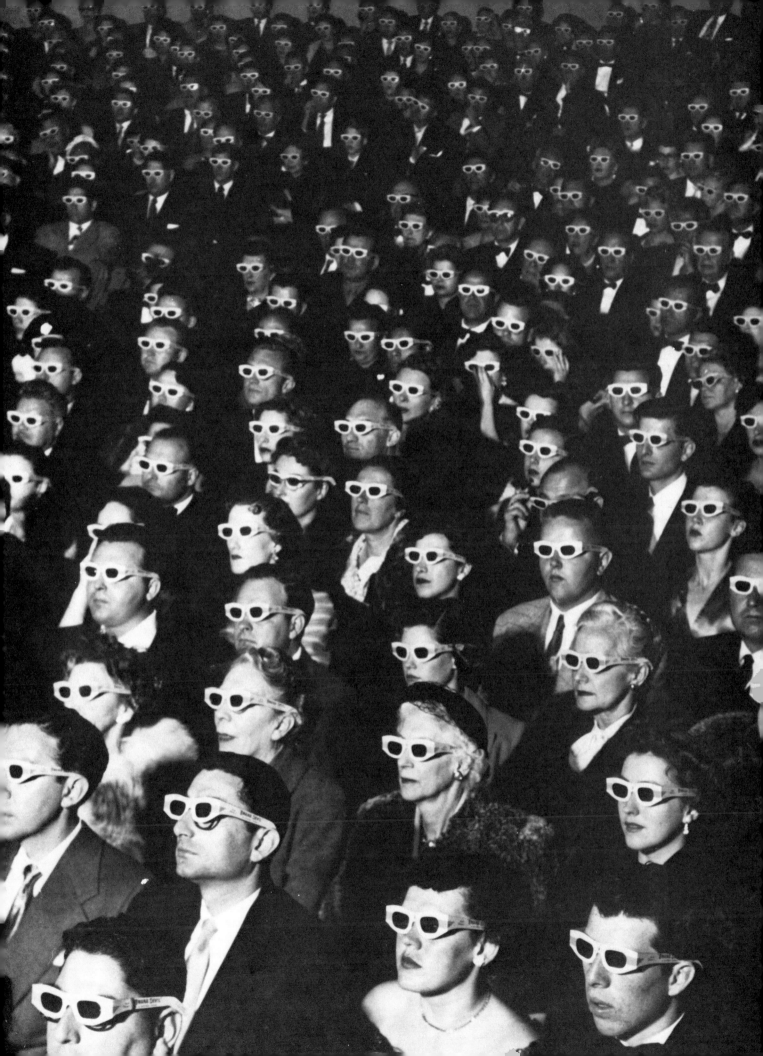

the film in which Robert Stack jabbed his rifle at the cameras.

Though not as refined as some of today's 3-D efforts, the original 3-D cinematography was not bad. Shot in Anscocolor and printed on Du Pont color-print stock, the high-contrast and pastel colors give an unexpected air of authenticity to the outdoor African scenes—surprising because most of them were filmed in the hills above Malibu in California.

The reviewers devastated *Bwana Devil.* They loathed it. Virtually every review of the film was bad. But despite the frigid press reception, the public went in droves to see the picture. At the Paramount Theater in Hollywood they lined up around the block four deep—right under the noses of the film executives who had snubbed 3-D. A critical flop, but a financial sensation, *Bwana Devil* richly rewarded Oboler's gamble.

For reasons perhaps different from Oboler's, the film industry was intrigued by the movie's popularity. In spite of its lame story, rough 3-D filming technique, and scorching reviews, the film drew capacity crowds wherever it played. It was this fascinating marriage of mediocrity and success that caught the studios' attention.

The slump Hollywood was suffering had affected the average and low-budget productions most severely, while the big movies—like *Quo Vadis* and *The Greatest Show on Earth*—were doing better than ever. Moviegoing was becoming a premeditated affair with the public instead of a habitual diversion. What was needed was an enticement to pull people away from their television sets regularly, so that the less expensive films could make money.

3-D had certainly done the trick with *Bwana Devil,* and for many of the studios that was persuasion enough in a time of crisis. By mid-December 1952 *Variety* was calling 3-D the movie industry's "Next Big Thing," and inside sources were reporting that almost every studio was working on some sort of 3-D system.

Warner Brothers was the first to come out in the open by contracting with the Gunzbergs for use of the Natural Vision equipment. Jack L. Warner had been the first studio head to use sound—back in 1929 with *The Jazz Singer*—and he wanted to lead the charge into 3-D. He also had a director on his lot, Andre de Toth, who had knowledge of 3-D and was anxious to do a 3-D picture.

De Toth had been intrigued by 3-D since the early 1940s—he wrote an article on the merits of the process for the *Hollywood Reporter* in 1946—and he wanted to make a 3-D film along the lines of an old Warner Brothers horror production, *Mystery of the Wax Museum.* He got the go-ahead from the studio in early January—in typical Jack L. Warner style: during a meal at the long table in the executive dining room, Warner glared at de Toth, shouted an insult, and said, "All you get is fifty days and a million and a quarter."

And so *House of Wax* went into production. Reporters had a field day with the fact that de Toth, the first director of a major 3-D feature, had only one eye. According to *Time* magazine, when de Toth was confronted with this fact, he replied serenely, "Beethoven couldn't hear music either could he?" The press chose to ignore the director's sincere belief in the possibilities of 3-D film—in their potential for involving audiences more fully in the experience of movies.

Even before the cameras were loaded for *House of Wax*, other studios started to move. Columbia was the next to put their money on the Gunzbergs. In mid-January they signed a contract to make three Natural Vision films during the spring. MGM and Universal built their own 3-D cameras, and Paramount bought the rights to a French system that had been designed in 1937.

By the end of January, as *Bwana Devil* steamrolled across the country smashing box-office records, four studios were shooting films in 3-D, and executives began to worry about being stuck with a backlog of flat films.

Industry observers watched the race to the next 3-D premiere. Just when everything seemed to be going in Warner Brothers' favor, Columbia sallied forth with a quick and dirty blow. Harry Cohn, the studio's head, halted the filming of *Man in the Dark* and had the script quickly rewritten for 3-D effects. The black-and-white film was rushed through production in eleven days, and Columbia slyly arranged for a world premiere in New York on April 8—two days before the much-heralded opening of *House of Wax*.

Man in the Dark is indisputably among the worst 3-D films of all time. Harry Cohn's system of judging

pictures by how itchy his "seat" felt was obviously overruled by his itchy corporate palms. Inept 3-D photography combined with an appallingly bad script yielded a picture eminently worth forgetting.

Man in the Dark did get some attention—though solely because of the novelty of 3-D. It was the first film to use extensive 3-D gimmicks—surgeons' scalpels slicing "through" the screen, bats, guns, even a car crashing out into the audience—but most of the effects were poorly handled. A roller-coaster ride with some potential for deep thrills was ruined by the cost-saving use of 2-D rear projection. With films like this in the vanguard it is easy to understand why 3-D was slow to find serious acceptance.

House of Wax premiered just two days after *Man in the Dark* and at long last brought the public a quality 3-D feature film. Though it was put through a speedy production schedule, *House of Wax* was made with care—and with proper 3-D techniques.

The film started out on a strong foundation: the story was based on *Mystery of the Wax Museum*, filmed in 1933 from a story outline by Charles Belden titled "The Waxworks." Screenwriters Don Mulally and Carl Erickson told the story of a sculptor hideously scarred in a wax museum fire who rebuilt his museum using hu-

OPPOSITE PAGE: A poster for *Man in the Dark,* the second 3-D feature film of the 1950s. RIGHT: Milton and Julian Gunzberg (at left and right) escort the Natural Vision camera off the Warner Brothers lot in a padlocked trunk during the filming of *House of Wax.*

Vincent Price, Charles Bronson, and Paul Cavanagh in a scene from *House of Wax*. Cavanagh, as a rich art patron, has just discovered the disfigured Price, whom he had believed dead after a fire. Bronson, as the deaf-mute Igor, is helping Price create a new wax museum.

man bodies covered with wax. The original production, starring Lionel Atwell and Fay Wray, was directed by Michael Curtiz. It was the last of the two-color Technicolor films; a year later the three-color process was perfected and first used in the 1935 film *Becky Sharp*. Though it met with negative reviews at the time of its release, *Mystery of the Wax Museum* now enjoys cult status among horror buffs.

When the decision to make *House of Wax* was announced, scriptwriter Crane Wilbur wasted little time on changes. He took the original script, altered a few characters and changed the format, and retained much of the original dialogue.

De Toth assembled a strong cast for the picture,

gambling on some talented newcomers. He chose Vincent Price for the villain, at a time when Price was not yet known for his considerable skill in the horror genre. Paul Piccerni played the young hero, and Phyllis Kirk the ingenue. Frank Lovejoy was given one of his first roles, as was Charles Buchinski—better known today as Charles Bronson—who made a memorable appearance as a mute.

The set design was simple and straightforward. The concept of the wax museum at the turn of the century was well suited to 3-D and was effectively laid out by the designers using a good deal of stage space. The wax figures were created by two Burbank artists, Katharine Strubergh and her daughter. (As a promo-

Phyllis Kirk is stalked on a foggy night by a mysterious deformed villain.

Phyllis Kirk helps her friend, Carolyn Jones, straighten her hat. After an unexplained disappearance, Jones turned up as a wax figure in the new museum.

Vincent Price tries desperately to stop the fire that is destroying his wax masterpieces.

Price amid the rubble at the end of the fire scene. While the cameras rolled, the local fire department arrived and hosed down the flaming set.

tion gimmick at the time of the film's release, the elder Ms. Strubergh offered to make full-figure wax portraits for only five hundred dollars.)

Filming began on January 19, 1953, using the Natural Vision equipment, and ended just twenty-eight days later, at a final cost of only $680,000. Even Jack Warner was surprised by the speed and efficiency of the production. After hearing the news he had a case of Jack Daniels delivered to de Toth's door.

The production cost included the expense of burning the wax figures—and nearly destroying an entire soundstage in the bargain—for the spectacular conflagration scene. De Toth had given notice that he intended to create the fire scene, but no one knew how serious he was. Rather than burning and filming in controlled pieces, the director chose to shoot the whole scene in one exciting blaze. He began by starting spot fires; one at a time the figures were ignited

and filmed. The three Natural Vision cameras mounted on huge dollies dodged each other in the excitement, then backed off to shoot the action as the entire set roared into flames. The fire eventually burned a hole in the roof, and firemen started spraying water on the building—and the set—while the cameras rolled. The only casualties of the adventure were the singed eyebrows of Vincent Price and the hole in the stage roof, through which blue skylight can be seen in the final cut.

Price's makeup for his after-the-fire face—grotesque even by today's standards—took an average of three hours to apply and was hideously uncomfortable. The actor's ears had to be twisted and bent, his nostrils twisted and flared, and his mouth filled with disfiguring dentures. The grim visage was the creation of Gordon Bau, under contract to Warner's and one of the most skillful makeup artists in Hollywood.

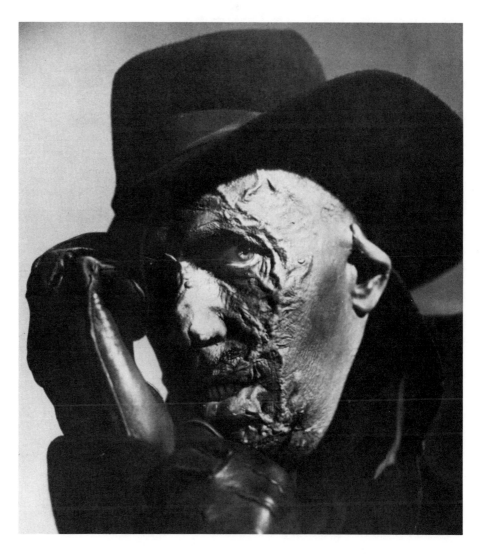

Price's after-the-fire face—the gruesome work of makeup artist George Bau

Phyllis Kirk discovers the mystery of the wax museum when she recognizes her missing friend as the wax figure of Joan of Arc.

Phyllis Kirk in the wax bath as molten wax from the vat above starts to pour through the tubes toward her.

Photography began under the direction of Peverell Marley, but, after he became ill during the first week of shooting, the job was taken over by Burt Glennon, with help from Bob Burkes—who went on to become Alfred Hitchcock's key cameraman. Lothrop Worth, the camera operator, and Howard Schwartz, one of the Natural Vision camera assistants, also moved on to become directors of photography.

The music in *House of Wax*, one of the finest soundtracks ever made by Warner Brothers, was composed by David Buttolph, with orchestration by Maurice de Packh. The score includes the particularly eerie "Phantom's Theme," which creeps in at odd times in the film, anticipating the horror about to unfold. In the initial release the music was presented in Warnerphonic sound, which used as many as twenty-two speakers to provide, through the soundtrack, an added illusion of depth.

Andre de Toth used 3-D in *House of Wax* to make a good picture better, and his concern for quality soon paid off with sensational results at the box office. In its premiere week at the Paramount Theater in New York,

The cast and crew during the filming of *House of Wax*. From left to right: Sam Goode, sound man; Peverell Marley, director of photography; Norman McClay; director Andre de Toth; a wax monk; Vincent Price (under the monk's hand); Jimmy McMahon; Phyllis Kirk; a wax effigy of Joan of Arc

The Los Angeles Paramount theater during the twenty-four-hour "premathon" for *House of Wax*

the film took in a stunning $123,000. Warner Brothers gave it a little extra push in Los Angeles with a twenty-four-hour "premathon" on April 17—kicked off with a "spook" premiere at one minute past midnight followed by an aircraft swing shifter's premiere at 2 A.M., a milkman's matinee at 4 A.M., a breakfast opening at 6 A.M., a career girl's matinee at 8 A.M., and other showings throughout the rest of the day. At the end of three weeks, *House of Wax* had brought in a million dollars, was the country's top box-office attraction, and was well on its way to becoming one of the most profitable films of all time.

House of Wax should have demonstrated the value of quality 3-D; in its early engagements it took in about five times more money than *Man in the Dark,* which was released the same week. Unfortunately, most of the studios did not analyze its success very closely. They saw money in 3-D, and in response sped up production schedules on their own sometimes shoddy 3-D pictures.

Columbia rebounded from *Man in the Dark* with *Fort Ti,* released in late May 1953. A historical saga of the French and Indian War, the film was an improvement over the studio's first effort, and was filmed in color, but it still fell squarely into the Grade B category. Only the fourth 3-D picture, *Fort Ti* did smashing business in its early weeks. For the first half of June

it was the country's top-grossing film, but competition quickly stuffed it back to its proper station—passable, but hardly a blockbuster.

Released with *Fort Ti* was the first post-*Bwana Devil* 3-D short, Walt Disney's *Melody.* Heralded as the first 3-D cartoon, *Melody* actually followed in the footsteps of the two animated shorts made for the 1951 Festival of Britain. The two earlier cartoons, far from being unknown here, had been making the rounds of American theaters during the winter and spring.

Melody was the first film in Disney's "Adventures in Music" series and was a highly stylized cartoon—probably influenced by French animated films of the time. The story follows the stages of life through pop-

George Montgomery trains his troops, the famed Rogers Rangers, in *Fort Ti.*

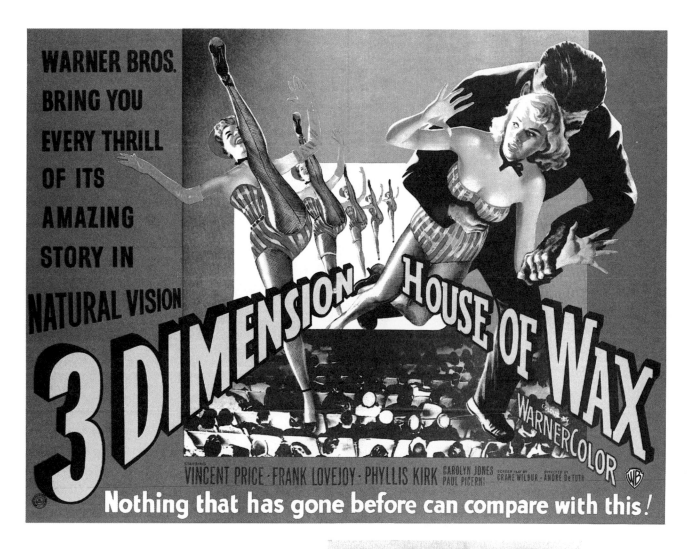

ABOVE: A 1953 poster for *House of Wax*. RIGHT: Poster for Walt Disney's *Melody*, the first American animated cartoon in 3-D

Walt Disney's *Melody* is a sophisticated 3-D cartoon, drawn in a style reminiscent of Paul Klee's work. It features none of the familiar Disney characters, but is fully worthy of the master animator's name.

ular tunes—from "Rock-a-Bye Baby" to the "Bridal Chorus" to "The Old Gray Mare," and ends with a trip to heaven accompanied by "Oh, Dem Golden Slippers." A month later Disney produced a second 3-D cartoon, this time in the now-familiar Disney style. *Working for Peanuts* featured Donald Duck and Chip 'n Dale in an entertaining story free of excessive 3-D gimmicks.

Universal was the next studio to join the race for 3-D profits. Their first effort, *It Came from Outer Space*, based on a story by Ray Bradbury, premiered in Los Angeles on May 27 after another speedy production job. In January, when the studio decided to try out the "depthies," they had assigned director Jack Arnold the twin tasks of overseeing the filming and contriving a way to shoot in 3-D without spending the money for the Natural Vision equipment, or competing for rental time on it. Arnold enlisted the aid of cameraman Cliff Stein, and together they built their own dual camera rig—not with two cameras facing an angled mirror as in the Natural Vision system, but with a pair of cameras side by side, one of them upside down. Arnold remembers the resulting equipment as a "big monster," but one that worked perfectly.

When shooting began in February, Universal required everyone working on the film to sign a pledge vowing not to divulge the nature of the plot or any of the dialogue until the film was released. The studio had a similarly secretive policy about its future 3-D plans—possibly because no decisions had been made.

It Came from Outer Space was photographed in black and white and then tinted brown to add a little class. Ads at the time of its release boasted that the film was shot in "scientifically perfected eye-resting Full-Sepia Mono-Color!"

Arnold cast Richard Carlson and Barbara Rush as a scientist and a schoolteacher who witness the landing of aliens in the Arizona desert. The heroes run into credibility problems—and the aliens even worse problems—when a landslide covers the spaceship. Charles Drake plays a local sheriff who has trouble accepting the seemingly tall tale until strange things start to happen in his town—disappearances and unearthly noises. Finally the townspeople help to free the rocket ship, which zooms away and leaves them to resume their normal lives.

Arnold showed considerable restraint by keeping most of the action behind the screen. As he explained in a recent interview, "I told them that I wasn't going to deliberately throw things out, just for the effect of doing it. Things that came out had to be motivated by the story—like the big telescope [see illustration

Richard Carlson and Barbara Rush get acquainted at fireside in *It Came from Outer Space*. (We observe the scene from inside the fireplace.)

What Carlson and Rush saw out in the desert: the spaceship crashes to earth, forming a fiery crater.

LEFT: *It Came from Outer Space* director Jack Arnold believed in natural 3-D effects. Here a telescope gently juts out of the screen as Richard Carlson and Barbara Rush contemplate space. BELOW: Unusual angles and good composition make the film a 3-D classic. In this scene Joe Sawyer helps Carlson tap a telephone line. OPPOSITE PAGE: A poster for *It Came from Outer Space*

above].... It was natural." During the avalanche scene that buries the spaceship at the beginning of the story, rocks do bombard the audience, but as a convincing demand of the plot. For the world premiere at the Pantages Theater in Los Angeles, catapults installed on the proscenium arch were filled with styrofoam rocks. At the height of the avalanche, the catapults were tripped. Arnold remembers the moment with glee: "That really set them off. These things were literally coming off the screen as far as they were concerned, and hitting them!... You never heard such screams in your life."

It Came from Outer Space drew good reviews and record crowds wherever it played. It easily replaced *Fort Ti* as the country's hottest film, continuing strong through June and into July.

After its string of smash successes, 3-D was more than ever the talk of the movie industry, and, as more studios started to jump on the bandwagon, it began to seem that the process really was the technology of the future. Industry analysts began to accept the possibility of a changeover that would be as momentous as the shift to talkies had been twenty-five years earlier. "Depthies" and "flatties" entered the jargon of the trade. But behind the big talk, most of the studios were

FANTASTIC SIGHTS LEAP AT YOU!
IN 3-DIMENSION
AMAZING! EXCITING!
SPECTACULAR!
IT CAME FROM OUTER SPACE
From Ray Bradbury's great science fiction story!
Starring
Richard CARLSON · Barbara RUSH
with CHARLES DRAKE · RUSSELL JOHNSON
KATHLEEN HUGHES · JOE SAWYER
Universal International
Directed by JACK ARNOLD · Screenplay by HARRY ESSEX · Produced by WILLIAM ALLAND · A UNIVERSAL-INTERNATIONAL PICTURE

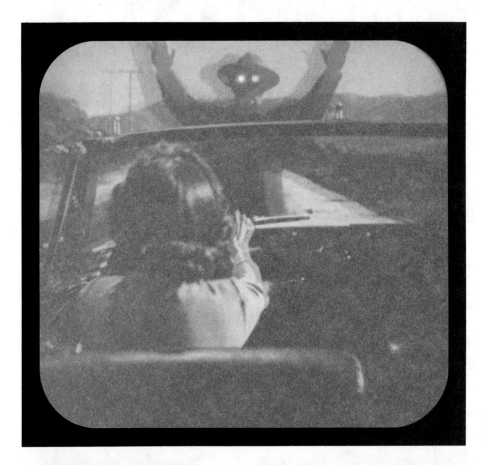

A weird stranger stops a car on the highway and kidnaps the surprised driver in *It Came from Outer Space.*

The aliens in *It Came from Outer Space* are able to take on human form.

still cautiously testing the wind, trying to decide if 3-D's success would last.

Paramount sent its first 3-D picture sailing in early June 1953: *Sangaree*, a colorful costume drama starring Fernando Lamas, Arlene Dahl, and Patricia Medina. In spite of the flashy ads and slick posters, the film was really quite ordinary. Yet tepid reviews were not enough to stop the public from donning their polarizing glasses once again. The film did well, certainly better than it would have done flat. It grossed nearly two million dollars before the end of the year.

Fernando Lamas, right, and Arlene Dahl, below, in *Sangaree*, advertised as "the picture with the famed biting kiss"

A poster for *Sangaree*

In mid-June MGM entered the field with *Arena*, starring Gig Young, Robert Horton, and Harry Morgan. Filmed in Tucson, with a rodeo background, it suffered from a very poor story. It was, however, the first film to use MGM's new camera rig. MGM, like Universal, had built its own camera system rather than pay the Gunzbergs for Natural Vision. Some magazines erroneously reported that the production men had merely dusted off the old *Audioscopiks* 3-D system, but the technical qualities of MGM's films, especially their second effort, show that the system was quite sophisticated. Unfortunately the equipment was crudely handled in *Arena*. The film made it onto the charts—barely—for a couple of weeks, but then disappeared into well-deserved oblivion.

Two more horror films came out before the end of

June—*The Maze* from Allied Artists, starring Veronica Hurst and Richard Carlson (the first actor to star in more than one 3-D picture), and *Robot Monster* from Al Zimbalist's Medallion. *Robot Monster* is regarded by many knowledgeable critics as one of the worst films of all time. After watching five minutes of it, one can easily see why. The photography, in black and white, is so amateurish, the sound so sloppy, and the acting so vapid that it is astonishing to think that the picture was ever shown in public. Some say that it was never actually released, but that it escaped instead. The lead is played by George Nader, who later graduated to larger budgets and some degree of success,

OPPOSITE PAGE: A poster for *The Maze*

THE **SHOCKING CHILLS** OF
THE SENSATIONAL SUSPENSE NOVEL
LEAP FROM THE SCREEN...in

3 DIMENSION

FILMED IN HOLLYWOOD U.S.A.

THE MAZE
The Deadliest Trap in the World!

PLEASE do not reveal the amazing climax to your friends!

ALLIED ARTISTS presents "THE MAZE" in 3 DIMENSIONS starring RICHARD CARLSON · VERONICA HURST with Katherine Emery
Michael Pate · Hillary Brooke · Executive Producer WALTER MIRISCH · Produced by RICHARD HEERMANCE · Production Designed
and Directed by WILLIAM CAMERON MENZIES · Written for the Screen by DAN ULLMAN · Based upon a Story by MAURICE SANDOZ

BELOW: Richard Carlson and Veronica Hurst in *The Maze*. RIGHT:
The creature from *The Maze* in a rare, never-before-published
photograph

The Indians attack in *Charge at
Feather River*. Warner Brothers'
second 3-D effort, the film is full of
action coming off the screen—
flaming arrows, tomahawks—even a
jet of tobacco juice.

The monster prepares for a knock on the head in a still from *Robot Monster,* one of the worst films of all time.

though in *Robot Monster* his acting shows little promise. As we watch his performance we find ourselves hoping that he held onto his job as a parking-lot attendant or whatever else he was doing to earn a living. The supporting cast is even less promising.

It is said that *Robot Monster* was made for less than ten thousand dollars—a believable figure, as no bad footage seems to have been edited out.

The title character is an alien, portrayed by a man in a very unconvincing gorilla suit, with—money not available for proper headgear—a fishbowl-type space helmet complete with radio antennae. The overall effect is, to be kind, ludicrous, and it could not have been taken seriously by the first audiences to see it in 1953. Its saving grace seems to have been that it was offered to theaters in a much more generous financial arrangement than were other 3-D films.

To counteract the damage *Robot Monster* did to the reputation of 3-D, Warner Brothers returned at the end of June with *Charge at Feather River*—the most gimmick-laden of all their 3-D films and one of the most fun to watch. During the Indian attack scenes, arrows are not just shot at the camera, they are thrown in huge bunches, as if the prop men grabbed handfuls and in a group heaved them toward the rolling film. In one of the most memorable scenes, Frank Lovejoy and another actor, hiding from nearby Indians, spot a rattlesnake creeping up on them from behind. Lovejoy, both brave and accurate with tobacco juice, spits in the eye of the snake—and into the audience— to scare it away. Fistfights, arrows, tomahawks, and bodies hurtling off the screen keep the audience weaving and ducking for the duration of this film, in what must be the zenith of 3-D's flying-objects phase.

While the 3-D effects were handled a little rowdily, the production quality of *Charge at Feather River* is

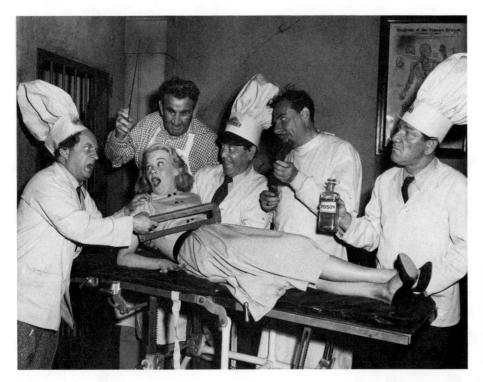

really quite good, especially when compared to other westerns of the fifties. In addition to Frank Lovejoy as a cavalry sergeant, the film features performances by Guy Madison as a frontiersman, Fred Carson as Chief Thunder Hawk, and Vera Miles and Helen Wescott as the obligatory white girls kidnapped by the savages.

To accompany the sudden wealth of 3-D feature films, a number of 3-D shorts began to appear. After Walt Disney's *Melody*, which played with *Fort Ti* and other Columbia pictures, that studio released two shorts featuring the Three Stooges: *Spooks* and *Pardon My Backfire*. Both are typical Stooges vehicles—the trio quite literally throws everything but the kitchen sink at the audience. *Spooks* finds the boys as detectives, hired to find the daughter of their employer. Their search leads them to a haunted house, complete with sliding panels, skeletons, knives, and flying pies and an ingeniously crafted bat with the face of Shemp Howard. *Pardon My Backfire*, the more refined of the two shorts, has the Stooges as garage mechanics; enter some crooks and a gun moll, and a battle ensues with the audience on the receiving end.

Universal made an eighteen-minute short of Nat "King" Cole singing his hit song "Pretend." It was first

RIGHT: *Pardon My Backfire*, the Three Stooges' second 3-D short, is one of the most effective gimmick films in the medium. In this scene the Stooges are attacked from behind by Ruth Godfrey, Angela Stevens, and Theila Darin. BELOW: A poster for Lippert's 3-D short of the 1953 Marciano-Walcott fight.

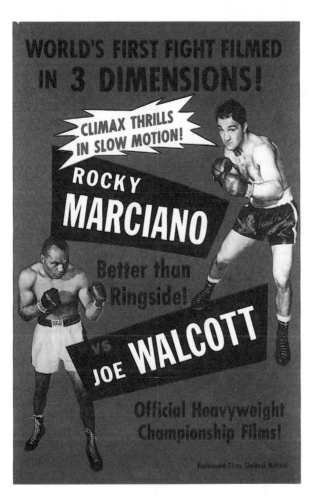

shown at the premiere of *It Came from Outer Space* in May. Cole's singing is punctuated throughout the short by various 3-D theatrics, including a slide trombone protruding into the audience and an acrobatic act, all in glorious black-and-white 3-D.

A short of the Marciano-Walcott fight was planned by the Lippert Company as a feature, but a quick knockout two minutes and twenty five seconds into the bout forced the producers to do some rethinking. They ended up by padding their footage out with commentary and releasing it as a seventeen-minute short. *Bandit Island*, also made by Lippert, was a less-than-sensational cops-and-robbers drama set in Los Angeles. It was ultimately worked into a feature-length flat film, *The Chase*, with the same cast and most of the same scenes.

From the animation studios, after the Disney pieces, came Woody Woodpecker in *Hypnotic Hick*, Casper the Friendly Ghost in *Boo Moon*, Bugs Bunny in *Lumberjack Rabbit*, and *Popeye, Ace of Space*. All four are good entertainments, though Popeye gives the most vigorous 3-D performance.

By late June 1953 3-D was at its pinnacle. In major cities viewers could often choose from among five

3-D films on any given evening, and 3-D had been topping the box-office charts for two months. Warner Brothers announced that all their future films, including *A Star Is Born* with Judy Garland, and Elia Kazan's *East of Eden,* would be shot as depthies. But alongside this blustery show of confidence strong pockets of resistance remained.

By mid-June *House of Wax* had run out of 3-D-equipped theaters to show in, and early predictions of a smashing $8-million take for the year were quickly revised downward. The film ended up doing incredibly well by any standard—number seven for the year, just above *Gentlemen Prefer Blondes*—but in June, when less than two thousand theaters nationwide could show it in 3-D, some studio executives saw a warning light go on.

Exhibitors also started to voice loud complaints about the quality of the 3-D pictures they were drawing and the stiff financial terms under which the films were distributed. Organizations such as the North Central Allied Exhibitors and the Theater Owners of New Jersey began advising members to boycott 3-D. Theater owners felt that they were being unfairly squeezed by the cost of installing special equipment, the union demands for a second projectionist at the 3-D showings, the cost of buying and distributing the polarizing glasses, and the unusually high fifty percent terms demanded by distributors. Compounding the fi-

nancial problems were the exploitive nature of some of the films, which hurt theater owners severely as patrons began to discriminate among the now-wide selection of 3-D offerings. One exhibitors' union blasted the worst 3-D films, claiming they had "antagonized large segments" of the public.

But the most critical obstacle facing 3-D lurked in the hopes of 20th Century-Fox to sweep the country by storm with a new wide-screen process, Cinemascope, in the fall of 1953. Inspired by the success of Cinerama, Fox had started investigating simpler wide-screen techniques, and through the efforts of research director Earl Sponable had purchased the rights to a patent for an anamorphoscopic lens—one that compressed a very wide image horizontally onto normal film, and expanded it again in projection. With a single projector, normal 35-mm film, and the Cinemascope lens, a theater could simulate the dramatic effects of Cinerama at a fraction of the cost. The major expense of converting a theater for Cinemascope lay in the cost of installing the extraordinarily wide screen—as tall as a conventional screen, but almost twice as wide.

With a sharp eye for publicity, the people at Fox talked up Cinemascope all spring. They pronounced it an even bigger "Next Big Thing" than 3-D, offered the special lenses free to other studios for use in their own Cinemascope productions, gave lavishly staged previews to the press, and privately beamed when

Two men are dwarfed by a giant Cinemascope screen, 20th Century-Fox's economy version of Cinerama. Cinemascope offered the spectacle of wide screen without the complexity of a multiple-projection system.

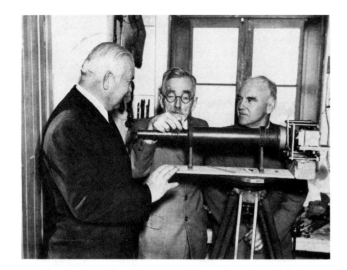

Inventor Henri Chretien (center) demonstrates a Cinemascope lens test to Spyros Skouros (left), head of 20th Century-Fox, and Earl Sponable (right), who brought the idea to the studio.

3-D produced such bombs as *Man in the Dark* and *Robot Monster*. For their first Cinemascope production, the studio chose a biblical spectacular, *The Robe,* and scheduled it for release in September.

Throughout the summer months the studios and theaters were left wondering about their futures. Most of the studios played a juggling act with a little of everything in their fall lineup, but many theater owners saw the situation as an all-or-nothing choice when they contemplated the expenses of converting their facilities.

July and August produced a slew of new 3-D releases, including RKO's *Second Chance* and *Devil's Canyon,* Columbia's *The Stranger Wore a Gun,* United Artists' *I the Jury,* Universal's *Wings of the Hawk,* Realart's *Hannah Lee,* and—confusing their own issue—20th Century-Fox's *Inferno.*

Though the studio's heart was certainly not in it, Fox managed to put out a reasonably strong 3-D entry in *Inferno.* The photography was competent, under the guidance of Lucian Ballard, the story well thought out, and the acting convincing. The film remains a 3-D classic.

None of the summer 3-D releases yielded glamorous results at the box office. They were overshadowed in July by *Charge at Feather River,* the top film for that month, and in August by a strong crop of flat films,

Robert Ryan struggles to escape a desert death in *Inferno,* 20th Century-Fox's first 3-D film. His wife, Rhonda Fleming, and her secret boyfriend, William Lundigan, try to do Ryan in by abandoning him in a desert canyon with a broken leg.

THE GREATEST LEAP IN 3-D HISTORY!
MYRIAD-WONDERED, CLEAR VISION 3-D
Brings The Technique Daringly Forward As It
Spans The Theatre From Front Row To Back Seat!

YOU are trapped in the great Devil's Canyon of the Mojave Desert!

YOU hang from a cliff and lower yourself into the valley below!

YOU are in the center of a thundering theatre-shaking landslide!

YOU are part of an overpowering, flaming love story!

The wonder of
3-D
STEREOPHONIC SOUND

The marvel of
3-D
Color by
TECHNICOLOR
ENHANCED A THOUSANDFOLD!

INFERNO

The most breath-taking man hunt that ever criss-crossed out of the screen!

Newspaper advertisements. At left for *Inferno* and below for *Second Chance* and *I the Jury*, a tough Mickey Spillane thriller that drew big crowds wherever it played

including *Gentlemen Prefer Blondes*, *Band Wagon*, and *The Moon Is Blue*. *I the Jury*, a black-and-white 3-D film based on a Micky Spillane novel, did very well in most cities, but with such stiff competition was not a sensational grosser.

Linda Darnell, as the ex-mistress of a New York gangster in *Second Chance*, is followed to Mexico by a hit man, Jack Palance. When she discovers her peril, she enlists the aid of Robert Mitchum, an American prizefighter. In this scene she cables for help as the killer closes in.

Second Chance builds to a stomach-churning climax aboard a cable car, where Mitchum and Darnell fight for their lives. Here their battle over, they ride happily to safety.

In *Devil's Canyon,* Virginia Mayo plays a notorious outlaw queen, the object of desire for five hundred convicts in Arizona's Territorial Prison. After a stint with a murderer, Stephen McNally, Mayo ends up with Dale Robertson, the man of her dreams.

John Ireland joined his son Peter (seen with Ireland here) and Joanne Dru to make *Hannah Lee,* a Jack Broder production.

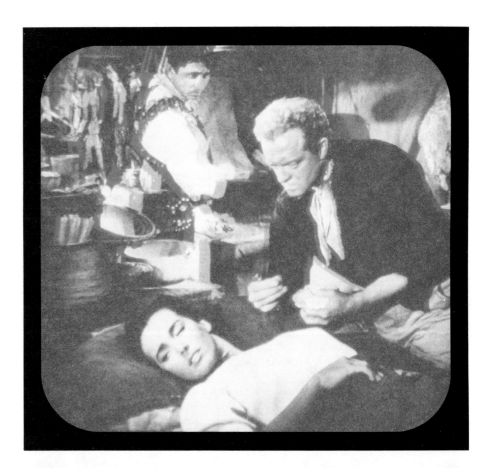

Julia Adams lies stricken after an attack by bandits in *Wings of the Hawk*. Van Heflin removes a bullet from her shoulder.

Randolph Scott, the stranger in *The Stranger Wore a Gun*. A young Lee Marvin also appeared in the film.

Jack Palance, after finishing *Second Chance*, returned in *Flight to Tangier*, this time as a good guy. Starring with him were Joan Fontaine and Corinne Calvet.

Rhonda Fleming, Gene Barry, and Theresa Brewer hoof it up in *Those Redheads from Seattle*, advertised as a "gal-stacked, entertainment packed" musical. OPPOSITE PAGE: A gala number from the same film. Guy Mitchell sings while the Bell Sisters do their steps. Agnes Moorehead had a minor role in the movie.

The sagging performances of the summer 3-D releases were noted in the front offices in Hollywood. Warner Brothers quietly took the 3-D tag off of the ads for *East of Eden* and *A Star is Born,* and, when pressed to disclose their plans, admitted that only three of their twenty fall and winter films would be depthies—a massive change of heart from the studio that as late as July had claimed to be making *everything* in 3-D. They did come out with a mild 3-D effort in September—*The Moonlighter* with Barbara Stanwyck and Fred MacMurray, a film well below the standards the studio had set with *House of Wax.*

On September 16, 1953, *The Robe* premiered at the Roxy Theater in New York, and its resounding success there—an incredible $267,000 in its first week—signaled the beginning of the end for 3-D. The studios had a new and more glamorous bandwagon to jump on, and one by one they started switching to Cine-mascope as *The Robe* smashed box-office records in city after city.

3-D did not die a sudden death, but fell into a lingering decline in the fall of 1953. With the studios uncertain about its future, theater owners were more hesitant than ever to install the equipment necessary to show it. And, with a limited number of theaters prepared to show their 3-D productions, the studios grew yet cooler to the medium. 3-D entered a cycle of stagnation, which *Variety* tagged "the new wait and see attitude."

Paramount was the first studio to return to 3-D after the release of *The Robe.* In a gesture that spoke volumes, the studio offered *Those Redheads from Seattle* and *Flight to Tangier* in both 3-D and flat versions. Previously 3-D films had not been available as flat films until they had played all possible 3-D engagements.

LEFT: Edward G. Robinson in the control booth of a television station in *The Glass Web.* Jack Arnold directed this murder mystery after finishing *It Came from Outer Space.* BELOW: A newspaper advertisement for *Kiss Me Kate,* a 3-D film version of the successful Broadway musical

The only other October release in 3-D was *The Glass Web* from Universal, starring Edward G. Robinson. Director Jack Arnold (of *It Came from Outer Space* fame) recalls it as a good picture that was most widely released in its flat version due to plummeting faith in 3-D.

With 3-D gasping what seemed like its last, MGM decided to perform a test of its drawing power. They scheduled test engagements in six cities for their new musical film *Kiss Me Kate.* Columbus, Dallas, and Syracuse would play the 3-D version; Evansville, Houston, and Rochester would show it flat. When the results were in, it was clear that the public had chosen 3-D. The cities playing the deep version did forty percent better business than those with the flat print, and all the 2-D theaters switched to 3-D as soon as the test week ended. MGM's head of sales sent a notice of the results to prospective theaters: "In the light of these experiments, we strongly urge theaters to play *Kiss Me Kate* in 3-D." Some discounted the results as unfair, because Polaroid had advertised extensively in the 3-D cities, and, in a crushing blow, Radio City Music

"3D!!!" THE FAMED STAGE HIT ...NOW A BIG COLORFUL MUSICAL!

Photographed in ANSCO COLOR Print by TECHNICOLOR

Kiss Me Kate

starring

KATHRYN GRAYSON · HOWARD KEEL

ANN MILLER with Keenan **WYNN** · James **WHITMORE** · Bob **FOSSE** · Bobby **VAN** · Kurt **KASZNAR** · Tommy **RALL**

Kathryn Grayson and Ann Miller, the stars of *Kiss Me Kate*, pop out of a 3-D frame.

Grayson with Kurt Kasznar and Tommy Rall in *Kiss Me Kate*. The movie is based on a musical version of *The Taming of the Shrew*, but the real action lies in the romances, counterromances, and severed romances of the players.

Hall decided to show the flat version at the New York premiere—citing the "shady reputation of 3-D in the public's mind." Yet most people in the industry saw the test results as proof that 3-D did have a place in the movies.

In its stage version *Kiss Me Kate* had enjoyed a long and successful Broadway run. The Cole Porter score included such classic musical numbers as "Too Darn Hot" and "Wunderbar," and the cast for the film included such stars as Howard Keel, Kathryn Grayson, and Ann Miller. *Kiss Me Kate* is an absolutely superior film in all respects, and it is not surprising that it became one of the top films of the 1953 holiday season.

Columbia returned to give 3-D another kick in the groin with two early November disasters, *Gun Fury* and *The Nebraskan,* and RKO brought out an equal disservice in *Louisiana Territory. The Nebraskan* was so bad that it provoked one San Francisco man to punch a theater manager in the face for subjecting him to the movie. He was fined two hundred dollars for disturbing the peace, but if the judge had seen the film he might have fined the studio instead. Apparently there were those in the movie business who would not be happy until they had crushed the last breath out of 3-D.

Phil Carey and Roberta Haynes in *The Nebraskan,* yet another Indian-fighting 3-D western.

Columbia forced Donna Reed, fresh from her role in *From Here to Eternity,* to go western in *Gun Fury.* This is how she looked in her 3-D debut. It was a terrible film, but Reed got to act opposite Rock Hudson.

Yet Thanksgiving marked the premieres of two more quality 3-D pictures to join *Kiss Me Kate*. *Cease Fire*—a serious black-and-white docudrama of the Korean War—and *Hondo*, a John Wayne western, with Geraldine Page, Ward Bond, and James Arness in one of the first performances of his career.

Hondo, distributed by Warner Brothers, was independently produced by Wayne-Fellows Productions in an arrangement unusual for the time. Warner Brothers contributed the camera system—a new one designed by their own camera department. The new equipment made it possible to film close-ups that were comfortable to view, something that had been a problem with Natural Vision.

John Wayne bowls his way through *Hondo* in admirable man-of-iron style. He survives torture at the hands of the Apaches, hurls a lance through a vicious Indian leader, and ends up with the woman of his choice. The 3-D stunts are kept to a minimum; the only time the audience really takes it on the chin is during a knife fight between Wayne and Rudolfo Acosta.

Some 2-D sequences are interpolated into *Hondo*. Apparently there were problems with one of the cameras—the lens was out of focus, the film broke, or something else went wrong—and, already in the can,

A newspaper advertisement for *Hondo*, John Wayne's only venture into 3-D.

John Wayne, riding dispatch for the U.S. Cavalry, comes to the aid of Geraldine Page and her son, Lee Aaker, who are besieged by attacking Apaches.

A bedraggled John Wayne takes a break during a rainy day of filming on location in Mexico. At left, the 3-D camera is protected from the weather.

John Wayne and Geraldine Page prepare to ride off into the sunset.

the footage could not be reshot. Instead the editors double printed the surviving negative and used it to replace the lost footage, so that at least there were two images to project. Though not three-dimensional, the scenes are short enough that they are not intrusive. The balance of the film is exceptionally well made, and the picture remains an outstanding example of 3-D filmmaking. The public responded to it in droves in 1953, and it roared along to become the second biggest 3-D movie of the fifties, just behind *House of Wax.*

Keeping up the tenuous string of top-grade 3-D productions, Columbia came up with a gem in *Miss Sadie Thompson,* which arrived at theaters just in time for Christmas, 1953. Harry Cohn, the studio head, lavished more care and money on this film than on most of his other efforts combined, and it shows all around.

Miss Sadie Thompson is based on Somerset Maugham's short story "Rain," which had enjoyed a successful Broadway interpretation in the twenties, and a film version with Joan Crawford in the thirties. Columbia's stellar remake put Rita Hayworth in the lead

role and included a second 3-D appearance by Charles Bronson.

The picture was filmed on an island in the tropics and made full use of the lush colors in the scenery and in Sadie's dress, hair, and makeup. The only suggestion of a 3-D gimmick is in a scene in which Sadie, in a moment of anger, sweeps some objects off her dressing table, and one of them bounces off the wall toward the camera and the audience. It has the look, however, of an accidental gesture. In another subtle segment, Sadie exhales a little cigarette smoke toward the audience. Both scenes come off so naturally that the effects could hardly be labeled 3-D gimmicks.

Miss Sadie Thompson was the first film to use the camera rig of Columbia's own design. They had used the Natural Vision equipment for their earlier efforts. Similar to Universal's system, Columbia's used two cameras side by side, one of them turned upside down so that the lenses could be as close together as possible. The film advance mechanism of the upside-down camera had to run backward in order for the two cameras to film in the same sequence. The whole de-

Rita Hayworth, as a steamy, free-spirited nightclub singer with a past in *Miss Sadie Thompson.* Stranded on a tropical island with a group of Marines, she leads a gay life, but inspires the moral indignation of José Ferrer, who sets out to reform her.

Rita Hayworth and Aldo Ray in *Miss Sadie Thompson*

Patricia Medina and the Queen of Tahiti comfort each other during a volcanic eruption in *Drums of Tahiti*.

vice was encased in a special soundproof blimp, or housing, making for a very large piece of machinery. But the flexibility and adaptability of the rig made *Sadie* one of the better photographed 3-D films of the period.

Not everyone who saw the movie liked it. Lloyd T. Binford, the eighty-eight-year-old censor in Memphis, banned it in his city. By his report, "This is the dirtiest picture I have ever seen—there isn't a clean spot in it. . . . It's rotten, lewd, immoral, just a plain raw, dirty picture, that's all. It should be banned with or without the filthy dance scene." It's safe to say that Mr. Binford overreacted. Most viewers in 1953 found the film entertaining and well crafted, as do audiences today.

The fragile reconstruction of 3-D's public image, which had advanced so gingerly from *Kiss Me Kate* through *Hondo* to *Miss Sadie Thompson*, was easily shattered by a pair of losers—*Cat Women of the Moon* from Astor and *Drums of Tahiti* from Columbia (yet again).

In February 1954 Universal returned with two more offerings: *Taza, Son of Cochise,* and *Creature from the*

Rock Hudson in *Taza, Son of Cochise*. With a little red makeup, Hollywood made him an Apache who rallied his tribe against the rebellious Geronimo.

Geronimo's form of Apache justice in *Taza, Son of Cochise*

LEFT: The Creature from the Black Lagoon gropes longingly at Julia Adams who swims out of range.
BELOW: A poster for the film

Black Lagoon. Taza was undistinguished, and it didn't get very far with the public, but *Creature from the Black Lagoon* was a winner. Directed by Jack Arnold (*It Came from Outer Space, The Glass Web*), it tells the story of a fish/man in the Amazon River that attacks the scientists trying to study it.

Once again Arnold, who had built a special camera for *It Came from Outer Space*, had to solve some serious technical problems before starting a film. The two biggest ones in *Creature* were how to get a 3-D camera rig underwater, and how to get the creature itself to *stay* underwater.

Clifford Stein devised a unique solution to the camera problem by putting two small 35-mm Ariflex cameras in a compact, watertight housing. Ariflex cameras were not in wide use in Hollywood in the fifties; most cameramen felt that such a small camera was not "good enough" for Hollywood films. But Stein was

advanced in his thinking, and when he found that the small camera was suited to the job, he used it—with very good results.

The problem of the creature was a little more ticklish. Rico Browning, the lead creature, was fitted with a suit designed to be formfitting, much like a wet suit, cast in a kind of foam rubber. Browning was an Olympic swimmer, able to hold his breath for up to four minutes while maneuvering strenuously underwater. With the suit on he was supposed to be able to dive about freely, but in the first tests he found that he could only bob around at the surface. The foam suit made him far too buoyant. A formfitting lead vest was quickly devised to fit around the chest and stomach area under the costume, making the creature slightly heavier than water. This neutral buoyancy allowed Browning to swim with ease, without having to struggle to stay down or go up. Precise buoyancy control was managed by the amount of air in the lungs, and a reserve tank of air was always available just out of camera range for whenever Rico needed it. He had to be careful, though, not to let any air leak from his mask into the foam suit when he took a breath. Otherwise, air bubbles slowly streamed out in a decidedly un-creature-like way.

Creature from the Black Lagoon was the first 3-D feature film shown publicly in a single-strip projection system, as opposed to the double-strip, double-projector systems that were the norm through 1953. When resistance to 3-D began to mount in the summer of 1953, a lot of attention was given to systems that combined stereo images on a single strip of film—the pairs stacked one above the other in alternating frames, or printed as Vectographs by Polaroid's process (described on page 30). Either system dramatically simplified the projection of 3-D films, eliminating both the need for theaters to hire an extra projectionist and many of the opportunities for projection error. Untrained projectionists were able to wreak havoc on 3-D films in the two-projector system, by misaligning the two images or showing them out of synchronization; the resulting eyestrain and headaches were often blamed on the glasses or on the films themselves, and kept patrons away from 3-D in droves.

Vectographs never got off the ground commercially. Polaroid played wait and see through 1953, missing its chance to set 3-D technology on a first-class footing,

as well as its bid to control the 3-D film-processing market. In January 1954 the company finally made its move, announcing a joint venture with Technicolor to develop a viable color Vectograph processing system. As it turned out, the venture coincided with the last dribble of 3-D productions; the plummeting volume of business killed the research effort before it even got started.

Two other single-strip systems relied on simpler technology: combining the two camera shots on a single strip of film in alternating frames and projecting the strip through a device that cross-polarized the two images and superimposed them on the screen. Nord brought out the first such system, and by the fall of 1953 many of the studios had made arrangements to use it, though none of the prospective clients got beyond the testing stage.

Moropticon was next. It was the invention of Boris Morros, and with a boost from Pola-Lite—the projection attachment was offered to theaters free with a large order of Pola-Lite glasses—the system gained a solid footing. Beginning in March, Universal offered both *Taza, Son of Cochise* and *Creature from the Black Lagoon* in Moropticon single-strip form. United Artists and Fox soon followed suit.

Three more big 3-D movies arrived during February 1954. Paramount brought out *Money from Home*, a

A newspaper advertisement for *Money from Home*

Dean Martin and Jerry Lewis romp, a follow-up to the pair's 1953 2-D hit, *Scared Stiff*. *Money from Home* leapt onto the charts after a combined 2-D and 3-D release and ended the year with a record nearly matching the smash success of *Hondo*. RKO released the Jane Russell showcase *The French Line*, despite a negative ruling on the film's acceptability by the Production Code, the self-imposed watchdog agency of the film industry. The decision to bring out the film without changes in spite of the ruling was highly unusual and generated a flurry of controversy. The film was banned in Chicago and many other cities, but its notoriety boosted attendance where it did play.

Money from Home stills. At left, Jerry Lewis with Pat Crowley. Below, Dean Martin with Marjie Millar. OPPOSITE PAGE: A poster for *The French Line*. Need we say more?

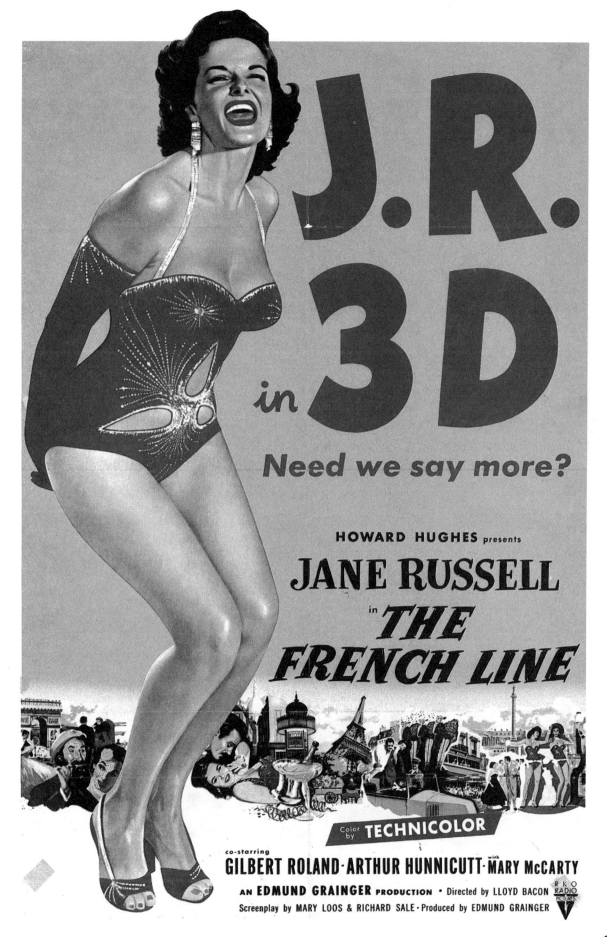

Gilbert Roland up against Jane Russell in *The French Line*

Jane Russell sings "Lookin' for Trouble" in *The French Line*. She found it, too, when censors objected to her skimpy costume and kept the film from playing in many cities.

Warner Brothers rounded out the month with *Phantom of the Rue Morgue*, their sorriest 3-D entry, but still a passable picture. Occasional 3-D shock shots—of a knife thrower, an acrobat, and the phantom himself reaching out of the screen—enliven the mediocre production, but the dialogue is so miserable that it transforms the movie from a horror story into a comedy. In spite of its drawbacks, the film pulled enough people in to break even, and it is still worth seeing for a mild chuckle.

By the early spring of 1954 3-D films were on their last legs. None of the studios would admit to plans for future productions, and one by one they brought out the last of their offerings already in the can.

Columbia washed its hands of 3-D with the release of *Jesse James vs the Daltons* and *The Mad Magician*. The latter film was a shameless rip-off of *House of*

A still from *Phantom of the Rue Morgue* shows good use of 3-D depth, with action in three distinct planes. Shown with the gorilla are Anthony Caruso, Karl Malden, and Patricia Medina. ABOVE: A newspaper advertisement for the film

A poster for *The Mad Magician*, Columbia's dismal imitation of *House of Wax*. By the spring of 1954 Vincent Price had earned himself the title "Mr. 3-D."

Wax, stealing Vincent Price, and both the writer and producer of the Warner Brothers project. The result was clumsily put together and in no way approached the quality or success of the original.

Paramount bowed out with *Jivaro*, RKO with *Dangerous Mission*, and United Artists with *Southwest Passage* and *Gog*, quietly allowing a number of previously announced 3-D pictures to flatten or disappear, among them *The Diamond*, *Camels West*, and *Ring Around Saturn*. 3-D fans probably didn't miss much.

Fox, perhaps wondering if there wasn't something in 3-D after all, released *Gorilla at Large* in May. The impressive cast included Raymond Burr, Cameron Mitchell, Ann Bancroft, Lee Marvin, Peter Whitney, and

Lee J. Cobb as the venerable police detective. The story is transparent, but the characters are so interesting that one ignores the plot and just enjoys the performers as they wend their way through the plodding story line. The photography is good, and in an original print the color is excellent.

Warner Brothers, the studio that had brought out the finest 3-D films of all—from *House of Wax* to *Charge at Feather River* to *Hondo*—signed off in fitting style with an all-time classic, Alfred Hitchcock's *Dial M for Murder*. Originally 3-D had not been planned for the production, but the studio felt that, since the film was an adaptation of a stage play that had used only one set, something extra was needed to overcome the

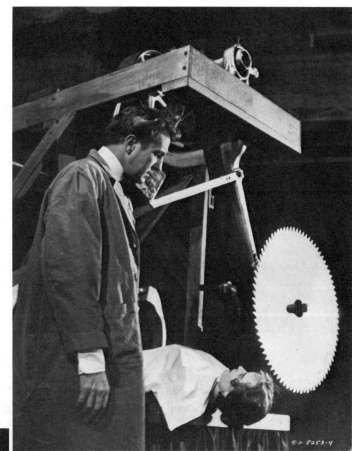

Vincent Price onstage, below, and backstage, right, in *The Mad Magician*. A terrible script makes this a hard movie to sit through.

Dangerous Mission put Vincent Price back in depth once again. Here he gets a briefing with Piper Laurie and Victor Mature.

Barbara Lawrence is kidnapped by the Dalton gang in *Jesse James vs the Daltons*.

visual restrictions inherent in the work. 3-D was elected and, by some accounts, was pushed on Hitchcock.

Alfred Hitchcock was not known for backing away from new technology; on the contrary, he had a history of using special effects, exploring rear-screen projection, matte, and other techniques that enabled him to present his material in unusual ways. In *Dial M for Murder*, Hitchcock handled 3-D in his own masterful style. Every shot was carefully composed so that, with proper camera movement and very precise convergence, virtually error-free 3-D was achieved. Hitchcock's daring use of unusual techniques makes this a landmark 3-D film—many of the effects have never been equaled.

Dial M for Murder contains three outstanding examples of 3-D virtuosity. First are the tight "macro" close-ups on wristwatches and, second, the suspenseful ultraclose shot of a telephone dial as Ray Milland's right index finger pokes into the number 6 hole, the "M." Both shots were faked.

With the 3-D camera systems available at the time the film was made, it was impossible to achieve the type of tight close-up Hitchcock felt he needed to enhance his story. He had, for virtually the same technical reasons, used a similar device in *Spellbound* (1945), for a scene in which Ingrid Bergman was held at gunpoint: Hitchcock's solution to having both the gun (in the foreground) and Ms. Bergman (in the background) in focus was to have a giant hand hold the gun. The same giant-prop technique was applied to *Dial M for Murder*, making it possible to manage ultraclose-ups without inflicting eyestrain, and demonstrating Hitchcock's undisputed genius for outwitting the limitations of the mechanical devices he worked with. Inasmuch as the effects are unnoticed—the prime goal of special effects—they are absolutely successful.

The third example of 3-D brilliance in *Dial M for Murder* was the considerable use of rear-screen projection, which Hitchcock resorted to for cost-saving reasons. Rear screen was avoided in most 3-D films because it can be easily detected by viewers, but in *Dial M for Murder* the visual blending was managed so well that the rear screen is totally unobtrusive. When viewed in 2-D, these highly inventive and well-executed shots cannot be appreciated.

Hitchcock's most obvious and effective 3-D moment comes during the murder itself. As the murderous in-

Alfred Hitchcock with the giant telephone used in the filming of *Dial M for Murder*. In order to make 3-D close-up shots with the background scenes in focus, Hitchcock used several giant props. A huge finger was built to dial this telephone.

A poster for *Dial M for Murder*, one of the last 3-D films of the 1950s, but one of the best as well.

truder attempts to strangle Grace Kelly, she is forced back across her desk, and her frantic hand thrusts out at the audience as she tries to reach the scissors to defend herself. Hitchcock triumphs again.

Dial M for Murder was released in the waning days of the 3-D era, and it did not get much exposure in its deep version. It premiered flat in New York, and most theaters around the country followed that lead, although at least one exhibitor, in St. Louis, showed it in full depth.

Jack Arnold and Universal trotted out 3-D one final time with *Revenge of the Creature*, the only 3-D release of 1955 and the last one for many years to come. The costume used in *Creature from the Black Lagoon* was refined for the sequel, and the story line

was developed to give the creature a bit more personality and more complicated patterns of behavior. A totally new cast was selected, including Clint Eastwood, then unknown, in a short splash-on role.

Some of the same problems that beset the first film remained: air bubbles, clearly visible in some shots, continued to issue from the top of the creature's head. However, the underwater photography was improved considerably. The crew had had time to evaluate the results of their work in *Creature from the Black Lagoon* and to refine their techniques for the return production. There are a few more gimmick shots in the sequel, but they are well integrated into the story. The scenes in the tank—in the sequel the creature was captured and brought to Florida for display—were shot at Marine-

The Creature walks toward the sea in the final scene of *Revenge of the Creature*.

land and are excellent, taking full advantage of the 3-D process underwater. The production was shot in black and white, a choice that baffles many in hindsight, as underwater photography in 3-D *and* color seems an absolute natural.

There were actually three different creatures in this film: Rico Browning did most of the strenuous underwater work, especially at the beginning, a stunt man stepped in for the out-of-water sequences in which the creature runs amok, flipping over cars and carrying off maidens, and John Lamb was employed for the scenes shot in the tank at Marineland. Lamb had been a cameraman on underwater sequences in the popular Lloyd Bridges television series "Sea Hunt."

Except for an occasional near-drowning among the actors playing the creature, the filming of *Revenge of the Creature* went smoothly. Very good 3-D was achieved through careful and selective camera placement and action, a result at least in part of experience gained during the making of *Creature from the Black Lagoon*.

In the final moments of the sequel, the creature is chased into the ocean by a vigilante mob. As he sinks from sight, the film ends, and with it 3-D's most glorious era.

3-D had been crippled by inferior exploitation films in its vulnerable early days, stifled by greedy distributors who antagonized exhibitors with unfair financial terms, further damaged by untrained projectionists who inflicted needless eyestrain on audiences, and finally eclipsed by Cinemascope, which grew to be the movie industry's shining star in 1954. The passing of 3-D movies marks one of the greatest missed opportunities in recent memory, a sad loss for a whole generation which has grown up unaware of the rapture of the depthies.

PAUL TERRY'S

MIGHTY MOUSE

in MEN OF SOLA!

FOR THREE DAYS, THE FIRE PLANET, SOLA, FALLS CLOSER AND CLOSER TO EARTH, BRINGING WITH IT THE EVENTUAL DESTRUCTION OF THE WORLD! TERRYTOWN'S LEADING ROCKET SCIENTISTS WORK FEVERISHLY IN AN ATTEMPT TO PERFECT THEIR NEW COMBAT SPACE SHIP, WHEN SUDDENLY...

BOOM

4.

SUPERMAN BREAKS LOOSE

Comic Books Join the Charge

In the summer of 1953, as the 3-D movie wave was approaching its crest, 3-D printing began to flood the newsstands. Anaglyphic 3-D advertising appeared in the *Los Angeles Times*, the *Boston Globe*, London's *Picture Post*, and the Wisconsin *Waukesha Freedman*. *Stars and Stripes*, the newspaper for U.S. soldiers stationed overseas, stuck a pair of glasses in a special issue and printed a 3-D article featuring a still from *Those Redheads from Seattle*. The folks back home got an even bigger thrill with the first issue of *3-D Movie Magazine*, which ran an ultradimensional photograph of Marilyn Monroe dancing cheek to cheek with Walter Winchell. *Popular Science Monthly* included a 3-D article on how to run a buzz saw. Thriftily, they left out the glasses and instead showed readers how to make their own using filters of gelatin and food coloring.

All these publications were printed from stereo photographs using techniques that had been developed decades earlier. Some were even printed by American Colortype, a firm that had been in the 3-D printing business since the 1920s. But when hand-drawn 3-D comic books hit the newsstands in early July 1953, the world saw something new.

Mighty Mouse was the first to appear, in an action-packed comic full of meteors and nasty cats from outer space. The added dimension opened a world of new directions in which the little mouse could fling his ene-mies. Published by St. John Publishing Company, by special arrangement with Terrytoons, the 3-D Mighty Mouse provided the first public demonstration of a process invented by Joe Kubert and Norman Maurer, two young comic-book artists. Kubert and Maurer were friends from childhood in New York, where they had shared an early passion for cartooning. Each had started taking commercial work before the age of twelve.

In 1950 Kubert joined the Army, and, while stationed in Germany the next year, he came across a German movie magazine with red and blue anaglyphic photographs and glasses. He was immediately struck by the possibilities for using the effect in comic books.

Mighty Mouse was the star of the first 3-D comic book, created by Joe Kubert and Norman Maurer in the spring of 1953.

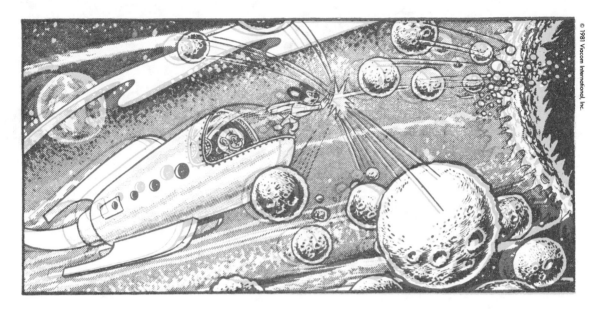

Mighty Mouse used the extra dimension when he punched asteroids . . .

After his discharge from the Army in 1952, Kubert approached Archer St. John—an innovative young publisher—with ideas for some new comic books, including one based on the character Tor, which Kubert had developed while in the service. St. John was interested, and the two entered into a co-publishing arrangement. Kubert handled the writing, drawing, and production; St. John paid the bills; and both men shared in the profits. It was a good arrangement for a young artist at a time when most people in the field were drawing for a low page rate.

With high hopes for the success of his new character, and with the knowledge that he was now in a position to test 3-D comics, Kubert asked Norman Maurer to join in the venture. Maurer was living in California, married to the daughter of one of the Three Stooges, but with some coaxing he was persuaded to move to New Jersey, where Kubert had set up a studio.

In the early spring of 1953 the two began to draw for St. John. They started with a book featuring Tor and a cartoon version of the Three Stooges and then began to experiment in earnest with 3-D. Their challenge was to draw and manufacture a high-quality 3-D comic book at a price competitive with the full-color ten-cent comics that were then the standard. With the help of Norman's brother Lenny, who had an interest in science and mechanics, they attacked the problem.

They determined where to have the glasses made and how to insert them in the books. They chose printing inks to work with the colored filters of the glasses and developed a simple and efficient method of making drawings. It was in this crucial step of preparing the drawings that they brought real innovation to the field of comic books (though their claim to the invention would later be challenged in a patent dispute).

Film animation studios had long worked with acetate cells as a labor-saving device. Using the cells, only certain parts of the artwork had to be redrawn for each exposure, and other acetate layers could be easily shifted in measured steps to yield the effect of motion. It required only a small leap of the imagination to create stereo cartoons with the acetate cells, as the various layers could, without too much trouble, be spread apart in space and photographed using normal stereo techniques. Tru-Vue had made 3-D cartoon strips since the late 1930s using this method, and several comic-book companies, including E.C. Comics, had experimented with the process, but found it uneconomical. The obstacle lay mainly in the way comic-book publishing was organized; the artwork was prepared at the publisher's office or in the artist's studio, and the camerawork was done by the printer. Either time-consuming, elaborately lit setups had to be made at the printer's, or the publisher had to invest in camera equipment.

. . . and when he tossed aside nasty cats.

Kubert and Maurer neatly bypassed the problem by putting two sets of carefully placed peg holes in the acetate sheets. Using their keying system the printer could photograph all the layers sandwiched together as a flat piece of art, then easily and accurately shift the layers to the left and right in order to photograph the second view of the stereo pair. The artist had only to leave some overlap in the background layers—so that gaps wouldn't appear after the shift—and create an opaque backing for the foreground objects—so that the background wouldn't show through.

Kubert and Maurer named their system the 3-D Illustereo process, hired a lawyer to file a patent for it, and formed a company—the American Sterographic Corporation—to sell licenses. They decided to give St. John first shot at the process, after which they would make it available to other publishers. They prepared two sets of sample pages—one set featuring the new character Tor, and the other the Three Stooges. A fellow artist, Bob Beane, drew a third set, using halftone shading, of a bathing beauty at the beach. (Beane moved on, in the 1960s, to head Wilde Productions, a major animation studio.) The three sets of samples were brought in to show Archer St. John. St. John went wild for the idea, just as Kubert "knew he would." He loved it and wanted to go into production immediately. But rather than using Tor or the Three Stooges, St. John decided to try Mighty Mouse for the

first test, as the little mouse had built up a loyal following over the years. St. John presented Kubert and Maurer with a book that had already been drawn, that was ready to go into production as a color comic, and asked the enterprising pair to convert it to 3-D and get it on the newsstands as soon as was humanly possible.

The two artists returned exhilarated to their New Jersey studio. Three days and three nights later, finished art in hand, they flew to Washington, to the plant of a printer outside the circle of New York trade talk. There they set up story boards, supervised the camerawork, and followed the book through a rushed production. The first printing of a million and a quarter copies arrived at newsstands on Friday, July 3, barely six weeks after the original meeting with St. John.

Despite its price of twenty-five cents, on racks full of ten-cent comics, the extra-dimensional Mighty Mouse was an astounding success, a virtual sell-out. Children loved the effect of putting on the Mighty Mouse Space Goggles to discover a magical world growing from the book's pages. Spaceships flew through space; explosions scattered flying debris; and asteroids came at the beleaguered hero from all directions.

When the sales results started coming in, St. John saw a bonanza in the making. He wanted to convert everything on his list into 3-D. Kubert and Maurer were assigned to produce 3-D editions of Tor and the

Three Stooges, and a staff was hired to redraw existing comics. By the end of August, St. John had produced five more 3-D comic books: the October issues of *Tor, The Three Stooges, The House of Terror, Little Eva,* and a new satire comic, *Whack.*

Tor had made his debut in the 2-D September issue. He was a super-strong, super-handsome caveman of a million years ago, who carried a cave monkey, Chee-Chee, on his shoulder. In the 3-D issue he continued his exploits, battling dinosaurs and evil cavemen with his strength and wits. Torchlit caves that fade into a murky distance, rocky outcrops, lunging prehistoric beasts, and Tor's active club, all provided opportunities for the artists to show off the graphic potential of 3-D drawings. In the first story, Tor is captured by an ugly clan of cave people and sacrificed to a "killer beast," a Tyrannosaurus Rex, which he manages to spear with a giant stalactite. In other stories he wrestles a giant turtle, escapes a destructive fire, and gives the reader a tour of his world, where "might is right," and "your life can be decided at the whim of a breeze . . . sniffed by the giant dinosaur."

Tor, the caveman superhero of a million years ago, was the creation of Joe Kubert, seen in a self-portrait inset on the opposite page. The opening story from the first Tor 3-D comic book is reprinted in part here and on the following two pages. The hero is captured by a clan of cave people and forced to battle a killer dinosaur for his freedom.

RETRIEVING HIS AXE, TOR WATCHES THE KILLER BEAST... NO MORE WILL THIS MONSTER HARASS THE CRATER PEOPLE!

Tor met more human enemies in his next issue—giants, madmen, and tyrants—and Kubert tried out a variety of panel arrangements, from tall, thin segments, to a two-page center spread, dubbed a "Panelrama." Through skillful blending of planes—a Brontosaurus in one drawing stretches through four levels, the breaks in its neck, body, and tail visible only with careful scrutiny—Kubert created a sophisticated stereo world.

As might be expected, the Three Stooges found zanier adventures. Their 3-D panels are crammed with sight gags and oddball graphics. Kubert and Maurer had drawn two Three Stooges comics in 1949 for Jubilee and had started the series up again with St. John in 1953. The 3-D October issue is almost too much for the eyes to take; every frame is crammed with the calamitous adventures the boys get themselves into. In the first story they take a roundabout trip to

the moon, along the way crashing a junkheap of an airplane after deducing that its propellor is the cause of a draft. The Stooges also make a showing as medieval knights in diving suits—Moe wearing an Ike campaign button—and end up in the water beneath the Olden Gate Bridge. In the November issue, also in 3-D, the Stooges are given title to Belly Acres Ranch and discover gold there—in Moe's teeth. Despite the obvious silliness of the stories, Kubert and Maurer clearly put a great deal of effort into the artwork. The depth in most panels was broken into five or six levels, and great care was given to every detail of draftsmanship.

The House of Terror proved to be St. John's only venture into the 3-D horror line, but not because the book lacked grisly effect. Though the cover is less than forbidding, young readers in 1953 must have known

BELOW: A 3-D bubble-gum advertisement, which ran in the first St. John comic books. OPPOSITE PAGE: The Three Stooges learn to fly in a page from their first 3-D comic book, drawn by Norman Maurer.

PICTURE OF EVIL

LIFE WAS A DRAB MONOTONY FOR HENRY CUSHING. HIS CHERISHED DESIRE WAS FRUSTRATED BY TWO INTENSE HATREDS. THEN ONE DAY HE FOUND THE POWER TO MAKE A STRANGE BARGAIN... ONE THAT COULD GIVE HIM EVERYTHING HE'D EVER WANTED.

they were in for a treat when they donned their glasses and looked into the gleaming eyes of Satan on the first page. "Picture of Evil," "The Violin of Death," "The Curse of Khar," "The Devil's Chair"—the story titles themselves are spine-chilling, and they are presented one after the other without so much as a Dubble Bubble ad to ease the tension. Evil curses, twilight mists, and walking corpses abound here, made even more chilling in 3-D.

Whack, St. John's answer to the just-founded *Mad* from E.C., contains spoofs of Dick Tracy ("Keyhole Kasey" by Chestnuts Mould), and Mickey Mouse (in "Mouse of Evil"), a love story featuring Scowboat Sadie, and a story about Maurer and Kubert titled, "The 3-D-T's". In this last tale we get a rare glimpse of the two artists drawing 3-D comics, or rather driving their workers to draw them. The last panel of the story is inscribed, "The End, thank goodness," the final touch added by an exhausted slave to 3-D.

House of Terror offered 3-D nightmares for those brave enough to put on the glasses. Shown here is artwork from the stories "Picture of Evil," opposite page, and "The Devil's Chair," above and right.

FOLLOWING PAGES: Joe Kubert and Norman Maurer drew themselves and their 3-D comic-book operation in the story "3-D-T's" from St. John's *Whack*.

A A LOOK BEHIND THE SCENES OF AMERICA'S SCREWIEST INDUSTRY!

118

AS CLARK GREW TO MANHOOD, HIS MOTHER DIED, AND THEN HIS FATHER...

LLISTEN, SON... I'M DYING...

NO MAN ON EARTH HAS YOUR AMAZING POWERS. YOU CAN USE THEM FOR GOOD!

HOW, DAD?

"YOU MUST FIGHT EVIL... CRIMINALS AND OUTLAWS. THEY MUST NEVER KNOW YOU ARE A SUPER-MAN!"

AND AS CLARK KENT WAS ORPHANED A SECOND TIME, HE KNEW THE COURSE HIS LIFE MUST TAKE...

A JOB AS A REPORTER ON A BIG NEWSPAPER WILL KEEP ME IN TOUCH WITH THOSE WHO MAY NEED MY HELP! I'LL WEAR GLASSES, PRETEND TO BE TIMID...

...BUT WHEN I'M NEEDED, I'LL WEAR THIS COSTUME, AND THE WORLD WILL KNOW OF... SUPERMAN!

The END

By August 1953 St. John was moving heavily into 3-D and had more than thirty people at work redrawing all the artwork on hand onto acetate sheets. Kubert and Maurer had also moved ahead with plans for licensing the Illustereo process to other publishers, though their lawyers were still troubling over the patent application. Power Publishing Company had purchased the first license, for a 3-D comic to be called "The Space Kat-ets," and E.C. Comics had expressed an interest. But in a disturbing turn for Kubert and Maurer, other publishers were preparing 3-D comics without consulting them.

National Comics was unabashedly proceeding with a large-format 3-D edition of Superman. After the success of Mighty Mouse, Jack Adler, the production manager at National, was asked if he could put out a similar book. Without a second thought he said yes, secure in his memories of the MacyArt books from his childhood that there was no great secret to 3-D printing. After a careful inspection of the St. John Mighty Mouse comic, Adler figured out for himself the method used to shift the layered drawings to produce the two stereo images, and instructed his staff artists in the technique.

Superman, In Startling 3-D Life-Like Action came out in September 1953 in an edition of over a million copies and proved a huge success. Though the stereo effect was far from elaborate—four levels of depth is the maximum—the star of the book was Superman, and National had cast him in some classic stories, including that of his origin on Krypton.

Harvey, too, published a 3-D comic in September; the now-classic *Adventures in 3-D*, which featured Harvey's own "True 3-D" process. Inside the front cover, the publisher described the "many years of research and experiment" that had been spent on the process in order to produce "a sensational TRUE-LIFE depth." Actually, the idea had come to Harvey just two months earlier, after the competition's success with Mighty Mouse, but Harvey had indeed come up with some new tricks.

Sid Jacobson, an editor at Harvey, saw a golden opportunity in a 3-D comic aimed at older children, a market Harvey was already serving with a series of mystery and adventure comics. Jacobson, Leon Harvey, and Warren Kremmer figured out the basics of the process, then went a step further by finding an artist who could make drawings that receded into the distance evenly, without being broken into flat planes. (In fairness to the history of 3-D, it should be stated that this sort of drawing dates back at least as far as Professor Wheatstone in 1838; and sophisticated stereo drawings had been made through the 1840s; also, a very simple example of a pole stretching from in front of the page to well behind it appeared simultaneously in the second 3-D Three Stooges comic.) A careful look through the pages of *Adventures in 3-D* reveals some unusual effects: a spaceship that spears back into the page, a leopard that leaps out toward the reader, and on the first page the word "THREE" angling back through the center of a "D."

For the artwork Harvey hired Bob Powell and Howard Nostrand. They were shown how to prepare the acetate layers and were offered twice the normal page rate for their work. The two split up the assignment, each handling two stories in the first book. Powell, assisted by Marty Epp and George Siefringer, worked in a studio in Oyster Bay, Long Island. Nostrand, twenty-two at the time and a former inker for Powell, had just set up his own studio in nearby St. James. For the background drawings the artists used

OPPOSITE PAGE: Clark Kent dons his Superman suit after the death of his father and sets forth on a career of battling evil. RIGHT: Harvey's comics broke away from the flat mode and included drawings that extended through space evenly. This example is from the first *Adventures in 3-D*.

ABOVE: An example of Harvey's *True 3-D* artwork. OPPOSITE AND
FOLLOWING PAGES: Howard Nostrand's story "The Hidden
Depths" from the first issue of *Adventures in 3-D*

a material called Craf-Tint, which, if wetted with a special fluid, gave shading in vertical lines and, if treated with another fluid, produced a darker cross-hatch shading. The acetate they used was untreated and would accept only a very thick, sticky ink. Nostrand, an extremely talented inker, remembers most clearly the aggravation of working with this special ink: "It was like tar," he recalls, and the artists had to wear cotton gloves to prevent smudging. They were given a tight deadline, and Nostrand often spent nights drawing on the acetate while his wife whited in the backs of his finished sheets.

When it was completed, *Adventures in 3-D* was an exceptional comic. The stories led the reader through some nice twists of the imagination: time travelers fought among themselves; the reader became a monster in one sketch; and every story featured an unexpected ending. The artwork remained consistantly strong, and the "True 3-D" touches helped to break up the cardboard cutout look.

YOU ARE IN ...

THE FORBIDDEN DEPTHS

WH-WHAT'S GOING ON HERE?

YOU'RE LOST. YOU DON'T KNOW WHERE YOU ARE, AND YOU STOP IN TIME AS A GUILLOTINE COMES CRASHING DOWN....

YOU RISE TO YOUR FEET--ONLY TO FIND YOUR HEAD DIZZY!

I--I MUST HAVE KNOCKED OVER SOMETHING! WHY IS IT SO DARK? WHERE AM I?

AN AXE!--COMING TOWARDS ME!

YOU RECOIL FROM THE UNEXPECTED ATTACK AND STUMBLE AGAINST SOMETHING...YOU WHIRL AROUND AND...

Y-A-A-H!

YOU RUN BLINDLY...FEARFULLY! YOUR MEMORY IS A BLANK! YOUR LIFE BEGAN THE MOMENT YOU WOKE UP! BEYOND -- THAT YOU REMEMBER--NOTHING!

YOU'RE LONELY TOO--LONELY AND CONFUSED! LIGHT--WHERE'S THE LIGHT?

WHERE AM I? WHERE AM I?

Y-A-A-A-A-A-H!

OF COURSE! THIS IS A FUN-HOUSE! I MUST HAVE STUMBLED IN HERE FROM THAT--THAT OTHER PLACE!

YOU PULL YOURSELF UP THROUGH THE EXIT, AND-- SEE ANOTHER PERSON!

MISS -- THANK GOD, YOU --

EEEEEEE!

AND AS YOU FALL, YOU GRAB AT ANYTHING IN YOUR DESPERATION, EVEN A *RUSTED CHAIN* HOLDING A HEAVY SWORD!

THAT SWORDS LIKE A *PENDULUM!*

IT BROKE OFF THE CHAIN! *HERE IT COMES!*

AGAIN YOUR LUCK IS WITH YOU. YOU SCRAMBLE FREE JUST AS...

IT'S NOT FUNNY ANYMORE! *NOTHING* IS!

LET ME OUT! DOES ANYONE HEAR ME? THIS *DOOR*...! I'LL OPEN IT AND...

ARRRGH-H!

YOU SCREAM AND BACK AWAY, YOUR MIND REELING! SUDDENLY -- A HAND REACHES OUT FOR YOU!

SO *YOU'RE* THE GUY WHAT'S BEEN SCARING THE CUSTOMERS! COME ALONG, MAC, I'VE GOT A GOOD NOTION TO --

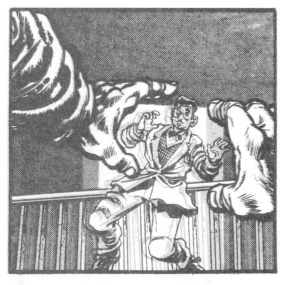

He vanishes into a doorway and you lose him. You reel and flounder! You're dizzy! You're lost! You turn into...

A SPOOK TROLLEY... COMING RIGHT AT ME...

You climb a narrow ledge! You're in a cold sweat...and even the door feels clammy! But what's behind it?

THAT'S HIM, OFFICER! OH--DO SOMETHING!

GET HIM! THERE HE IS!

You're confused...bewildered! You're the target in a chase! Staggeringly, you retreat into the house of horrors!

HE'S RUNNING THROUGH THAT OTHER ROOM! DON'T LET HIM OUT OF YOUR SIGHT!

You stumble towards a rear-stairway that suddenly pops into your memory. Then--as you throw open the door and look down at a cellar--everything becomes CRYSTAL-CLEAR!

NO ONE WANTS TO LOOK AT ME...TALK TO ME! IT'S BETTER TO GO BACK HERE WHERE I BELONG!

So you throw yourself into the bubbling vat--into the mother matrix that gave you life-- for you are a LUMP of WAX that came to life--only to find that DEATH was better than HATE and LONELINESS!

National's *Superman* cover

Harvey's *Adventures in 3-D* cover

Harvey stepped deeper into 3-D with the December issues of *True 3-D* (a sister publication to *Adventures in 3-D*), *3-D Dolly*, *Harvey 3-D Hits* (featuring Sad Sack), and *Captain 3-D,* a new character drawn by Jack Kirby. Harvey had high hopes for Captain 3-D, a superhero able to travel in "unseen dimensions," invented by one of the kings of comic book art. Early in his career, Kirby had joined with Joe Simon to create Captain America, and he had since come up with a stable of successful characters. Harvey contacted Kirby in the summer of 1953 and asked him to develop a hero to lead the 3-D boom. Captain 3-D was the result. Passed down through the generations in the *Book of D,* Captain 3-D came to life when viewed through the ancient glasses, fulfilling his mission to battle the forces of evil.

Unfortunately, by the time the captain reached the newsstands, Harvey was discovering the fragility of the 3-D comic-book market. St. John, as the first publisher in the field, was also the first to discover how easily success could evaporate. After the incredible ninety-nine percent sale of Mighty Mouse, St. John had plunged headlong into 3-D, with five October issues, and seven November issues, all with editions of more than a million copies. But sales, instead of gathering momentum as expected, began to dwindle instead. The second batch of comics, the October issues, yielded sales of only seventy-five percent and fifty percent, and the third batch, the November issues—which appeared with National's and Harvey's first efforts—showed miserable sales of thirty-five percent, twenty percent, and even ten percent. That drove St. John from the field. The final December issue of Mighty Mouse was a parting gesture. For St. John, a small business that had made a massive commitment to 3-D with huge print runs and a special staff of thirty artists, the financial losses nearly proved fatal.

National proceeded with much more caution. Their *Superman* was successful, but a single December issue—*Batman*—did not fare as well, so they abandoned the glasses and resumed business as usual with ten-cent color comics.

OPPOSITE AND FOLLOWING PAGES: Cover and 3-D artwork from Jack Kirby's *Captain 3-D*

130

132

3-D LOVE
STERIOGRAPHIC PUBLICATIONS
3D
L.N.
25¢
DEC.
VIVID...
DYNAMIC...
EXCITING...
CLOSER-TO-LIFE STORIES
in-CLOSER-TO-LIFE 3RD DIMENSION
FREE-3D
EYEPIECE ENCLOSED

3-D Romance cover

Sheena the Jungle Queen cover

Harvey managed to slide through the fall without serious damage, but there are signs that they, too, beat a hasty retreat from 3-D. Their November *Adventures in 3-D* and December *True 3-D* issues sold exceedingly well, each more than ninety percent, but the company viewed those results warily. They had taken on eight extra artists to put out four December issues, but that was their peak month. In January and February they published only one issue each of *Adventures in 3-D* and *True 3-D*, an ad for a second *Captain 3-D* that never appeared, and a pair of ten-cent comics, *The Katzenjammer Kids* and *Jiggs and Maggie*, which each included a single 3-D story, but no glasses.

The withdrawal of three publishers from the field did not mean the end of 3-D comics—not quite. A number of other publishers were busily preparing to give the idea a try. In December 1953 a spate of new titles appeared: *3-D Love, Jungle Thrills, Indian Warriors, Jet Pup, Sheena the Jungle Queen, Katy Keene, Felix the Cat,* and a number of children's cartoon books.

3-D Love, and the January 1954 *3-D Romance* were

the only 3-D comics made for older girls. Both were published by Steriographic Publications, a company formed by Ross Andru and Michael Esposito, and both are filled with surprisingly sophisticated stereo graphics. Inner thoughts and feelings are given a hovering presence in the distant background, flings in the city show up as a crazy collage of champagne bottles, dancing couples, neon lights, and maracas layered into diminishing space. The stories are sometimes unexpectedly sordid. A Viennese beauty marries an American soldier only to discover when he brings her home to Ohio that he is—horror of horrors—a factory worker! A gigolo's life is ruined, his heart broken, when he falls for a gigolette. A career woman lies and cheats her way to the top only to be stuck with a man who is as sly as she. Alcohol, full moons, treachery, and tragic endings swirl thickly through these, the scarlet ladies of the 3-D comics.

OPPOSITE AND FOLLOWING PAGES: Cover and 3-D artwork from *3-D Love*

WAS ALONE..., I HAD LOST HIM! OVER AND OVER AGAIN MY TORTURED BRAIN SCREAMED OUT, "DARLING, COME BACK! I NEED YOU SO! I'VE BEEN SUCH A FOOL! DARLING, PLEASE..."

FORGIVE ME...

I THOUGHT I HAD A WIFE... BUT I WAS WRONG! NOTHING'S GOOD ENOUGH FOR YOU, LUISE! NOT ME... NOT MY FRIENDS... NOTHING! AS FAR AS I'M CONCERNED, I HOPE I NEVER LAY EYES ON YOU AGAIN!

I SAT IN THE DARKENED ROOM, MY AGONIZED SOBS ECHOING HOLLOWLY IN THE EMPTY HOUSE--TRYING TO THINK, TRYING TO UNDERSTAND THAT SCREAMING FIGHT THAT TOOK PLACE AN HOUR AGO....

W-WE (SOB) WERE SO HAPPY ONCE! WHAT-- (SOB) WHAT HAPPENED TO US?

I COULDN'T HELP REMEMBERING HOW IT ALL BEGAN...IT WAS THREE YEARS AGO IN THE WEST SECTOR OF GERMANY, I WAS WORKING AS A SALESGIRL IN A SMALL SHOP...

ER...WEI-- VIEL, ER... SCARF...

DON'T STRAIN PRIVATE, I SPEAK ENGLISH!

IN AMERICA *EVERYONE* HAS *LOTS OF MONEY* AND *BIG HOUSES* AND *PLENTY TO EAT!* REMEMBER HOW WE LIVED IN VIENNA BEFORE THE WAR, LUDWIG...WITH *MAIDS* AND *CHAUFFEURS!* AMERICA IS LIKE THAT...*ONLY BETTER!*

BEFORE HITLER'S REGIME, MY FAMILY HAD BEEN A MEMBER OF AUSTRIAN LESSER NOBILITY. I WAS LOOKING FORWARD TO RETURNING TO MY OLD STATION IN LIFE...

LUISE! LUDWIG! HERE, DARLING! HERE I AM!

PETER, PETER! WE'RE HERE! WE'RE IN AMERICA!

AS WE CAME OFF THE GANG-PLANK AND PETER TOOK ME INTO HIS ARMS I WANTED TO CRY WITH HAPPINESS! I WAS HOME!

DARLING, HOLD ME! *HOLD ME TIGHT!*

LUISE, OH, HONEY, I THOUGHT YOU'D *NEVER* GET HERE!

WE SPENT A WEEK IN NEW YORK AND IT WAS EVERYTHING I HAD EXPECTED. BRIGHT LIGHTS, EXCITEMENT AND LUXURY! MY DREAMS WERE ALL COMING TRUE...

ON THE FOLLOWING SUNDAY WE BOARDED A TRAIN FOR NEWBURG, OHIO...

...YOU CAN KEEP NEW YORK! GIVE ME THE *MIDDLE WEST* AND THE *QUIET LIFE!* I'M *NOT* A BIG CITY BOY!

OH, PETER, YOU'RE *TEASING!* NEWBURG CAN'T BE THAT SMALL!

BUT HE WASN'T TEASING! NEWBURG, OHIO, WAS NOT AT ALL WHAT I HAD EXPECTED....

THIS IS IT, HONEY! *HOME SWEET HOME!*

I-IT'S CHARMING, PETER!

BUT IT'S SO DINGY, SO COMMON!

Sheena the Jungle Queen was a heroine tailored—or untailored—to the interests of adolescent boys. Her full figure and skimpy leopard-skin outfit must have had great appeal among junior high romeos. In a reversal of the Tarzan-and-Jane syndrome, Sheena had her Bob, a handsome klutz who required constant rescuing. Sheena's jungle reign began in 1937 and ran until 1953. The December 3-D issue was her last appearance, and she fought her way through it in a parting blaze of glory, dodging spears, swinging through the trees, and breaking up a slave ring. Sheena's disappearance in 1953 coincided with a growing movement toward censorship of the comics. Her shapeliness aroused the indignation of worried mothers, and forced her into early retirement.

Sheena the Jungle Queen ended a seventeen-year comic-book career with her 1953 3-D issue. Apparently her cutaway outfit was too scant for the Eisenhower era.

In another memorable one-time appearance, Katy Keene put on a fashion show in her only 3-D comic, published in December 1953 by Close-Up, an imprint of Archie Comics. Bill Woggon, her artist, was asked to work up flat art for a special 3-D issue, which would be redrawn for 3-D in Archie's New York office. This Woggon did, fitting Katy into costumes submitted by readers from all over the country. From her dresses down to her underwear—and even to her boyfriends' cars—Katy appeared as her readers wanted to see her. (Had she had veto power, she might have es-

caped appearing in a Jolly Green Giant suit, but Woggon had the final say.)

From the flat line art, Bob White, at Archie, prepared the 3-D version of Katy Keene. His treatment is limited to three levels, crude work compared to St. John's or Harvey's comics, but he did come up with an interesting effect by leaving plain areas of red and blue for sky, walls, and decoration. The colored areas certainly make the book the most attractive to look at without filters, but, seen through the glasses, colors take on a neon look, as one eye sees white and the other black. The red-and-blue patchwork technique is hard on a reader's eyes, but it does liven up Katy's surroundings.

Katy Keene's clothes were designed by readers.

The flurry of 3-D activity in comic-book publishing during the summer and fall of 1953 did not go unnoticed by American gum-card manufacturers, who were looking for enticing ways to sell gum to the same children who bought comic books. Before the end of the year, the young public had three 3-D gum-card series to collect: a set of antique automobile cards, from Bowman, and two sets of Tarzan cards from Topps, showing the stories from the new movies, *Tarzan and the She Devil* and *Tarzan's Savage Fury*. The Tarzan cards were extremely well produced, printed on a bright, coated card stock. They remain among the finest examples of anaglyphic printing. The drawings, by an artist whose name has since been lost, made fine use of stereo imagery within the restrictions of the small card size.

The *Tarzan and the She Devil* cards, following the plot of the movie, show Tarzan (Lex Barker) and Jane (Joyce MacKenzie) attempting to stop a group of ivory poachers (Monique Van Vooren, Raymond Burr, and Tom Conway) who kidnap an entire native tribe and force them to work as porters. Tarzan and Jane are also kidnapped along the way, but in the end manage to escape by calling in friendly elephants. Some of the best 3-D scenes are incidental to the plot, as when a butterfly floats in front of the jungle growth during one of Tarzan's many daring leaps through the trees.

The other, rarer set of cards, *Tarzan's Savage Fury*, pits Tarzan (Lex Barker again) against a Russian agent (Charles Kovin) who murders Tarzan's cousin and an English traitor (Patrick Knowles) and then impersonates the cousin in order to locate a diamond hoard that has great military importance. It is too bad for Topps, and for collectors of 3-D gum cards, that both these Tarzan films are among the weakest ever made.

A sampling of gum cards from the *Tarzan and the She Devil* set, published by Topps in 1953

TARZAN & THE SHE DEVIL—*the Laikopos are trapped*

TARZAN & THE SHE DEVIL—*waiting to strike*

TARZAN & THE SHE DEVIL—*Jane is trapped*

TARZAN & THE SHE DEVIL—*fight with a giant*

TARZAN & THE SHE DEVIL—*through the trees*

TARZAN & THE SHE DEVIL—*not a minute to lose*

By January 1954 publishers were drawing back from 3-D. St. John and National, as we have seen, made their last attempts in December 1953, and by January, Harvey was experimenting with limited 3-D issues at the standard ten-cent cover price. In the same month Atlas—an imprint covering the work of a number of publishers—tried their hand with a pair of oversize, full 3-D comics at the bargain price of only fifteen cents—complete with two pairs of glasses.

The two Atlas titles, *3-D Action* and *3-D Tales of the West*, offered rough, tough tales of war and adventure in limited—three level—3-D. The western book served up gunfights, brawls, Indians, and all-American patriotism. In one scene Big Jim Fraser stops a band of raiders from attacking a work party on the transcontinental railroad by punching their leader and giving the rest a speech. "He told them about the Railroad and about their country! He told them about his dream and their future! They listened—'That's what this Railroad means! It means commerce and Industry! It

Big Jim Fraser, foreman of a railroad gang, had a vision of America's future in *3-D Tales of the West*.

means America will be great. . . . There will be schools here, great cities, happy families, and good living. . . .'" When the moralizing ended, the raiders signed on as members of Fraser's work party.

3-D Action presented championship boxing, Russian spies, and combat adventure from Korea. In one leathery story Sergeant Socko Swenski explains how to take a Korean hill, first blasting the "Reds" on top with howitzers and mortars, then charging up with bayonets. When the "scummies" run, the bombers are called in to finish the job. As a final touch, "some G.I. pulls a flag outta his shirt and hangs it on a battered tree!"

These were pre-Vietnam times of American bravado, of patriotism frenzied by fear. The Russians had exploded their first atomic bomb in 1949, and while Americans dug bomb shelters under their lawns from coast to coast, the cold war stakes rose. In November 1952 a U.S. test of the hydrogen bomb destroyed the atoll of Eniwetok in the Marshall Islands, and just nine months later the Russians exploded their own H-bomb in Siberia. In October 1953 Senator Joseph McCarthy launched an investigation of the U.S. Army, which he suspected of Communist subversion. And in the national climate of fear and suspicion, the comics too came under attack—not as Communist propaganda, but as corruptors of youth.

Korean War story from *3-D Action*

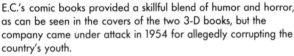
E.C.'s comic books provided a skillful blend of humor and horror, as can be seen in the covers of the two 3-D books, but the company came under attack in 1954 for allegedly corrupting the country's youth.

The two Atlas comics seemed to be making a conscious effort to remove themselves from the line of the coming attack, and, indeed, they each carry a tiny star on the cover with the legend "conforms to the comics code," an early indication of self-regulation and self-protection by the comic industry. During the spring of 1954 popular outrage against comic books reached a fever pitch. In April, in response to "thousands of letters," a U.S. Senate subcommittee investigating juvenile delinquency began to focus its attention on comic-books. In the same month Frederic Wertham's book, *Seduction of the Innocent*, was published to a great hue and cry.

Wertham's book is difficult to read seriously today, as its assertions are often wild and unfounded—that Batman and Robin, for instance, were homosexuals, and that Wonder Woman was a lesbian sadist—but

at the time it was read with great concern by parents across the country. A prepublication excerpt in the *Ladies' Home Journal* generated a flurry of letters, and women began to form censorship committees to blacklist comics and convince newsdealers to carry a more limited selection.

In the middle of the dispute, hoping it would all die away, sat the comic-book publishers. One of the prime targets among them was William Gaines, the originator of horror comics in the 1940s and the last to publish 3-D comics in the spring of 1954.

Gaines's father, M. C. Gaines, had been a comic-book pioneer in the 1930s; by some accounts he created the standard comic-book format. After World War II the elder Gaines formed a new company, Educational Comics, popularly known as E.C., which published a wide range of material, from Bible stories to adventures of the superheroine Moon Girl. William Gaines inherited the company in 1947 and, after a period of searching, began to turn the business on its ear with some radical innovations. In 1950 he launched *Crypt of Terror, The Vault of Horror, The Haunt of Fear, Weird Science, Weird Fantasy, Two Fisted Tales,* and *Crime SuspenStories,* in what he described as E.C.'s "New Trend" in comic books. Their success can be measured by the flocks of imitators that followed over the next few years.

Gaines had assembled some of the finest artists and writers in the industry when he launched his "New Trend" line—Graham Ingels, John Craig, Albert Feldstein, Harvey Kurtzman, and Wallace Wood. When the comics went into circulation they attracted even more artists to E.C.—among them Bernie Krigstein, Will Elder, Jack Davis, Frank Frazetta, Joe Orlando, George Evans, and John Severin. The comics they produced stood out from the competition like the apple in the Garden of Eden, and in the end caused almost as much trouble.

In 1952 E.C. introduced *Mad,* the invention of editor Kurtzman, and it swiftly grew into the wildest success story in the business. Gaines had turned his company—and the comic-book industry—around and onto a new track in the space of three years.

It is not surprising that Gaines wanted to try 3-D when it came along, nor is it surprising that he pursued a course different from that of his competitors. He had

long been interested in 3-D, even outside his business. He was one of the early owners of the Stereo Realist camera, and when 3-D movies started coming out, he went to every one, wearing a pair of specially made prescription 3-D glasses. In 1952 Gaines and Al Feldstein experimented with 3-D comics, using stereo cameras and three-dimensional setups, but they couldn't devise any practical production methods. Both men recognized the breakthrough Kubert and Maurer had made when Mighty Mouse was released, and E.C. purchased a license from the two innovators for the production of two comic books. As part of the agreement, Will Elder was sent to New Jersey for training in the Illustereo process.

At the same time E.C. undertook a patent search on its own, in order to be on firm legal footing when its first 3-D books were published. Before long E.C.'s lawyers located a patent granted to Freeman H. Owens in 1936 for a "Method of Drawing and Photographing Stereoscopic Pictures in Relief" (patent no. 2,057,051), which had anticipated in every detail the Illustereo technique. Al Feldstein found Owens in the Manhattan phone book and still remembers his response to the first telephone call. In a dry voice he said, "I was wondering when one of you guys would call."

Though the patent would remain effective only through October 13, 1953—seventeen years being the legal duration of patents—E.C. bought it from Owens and promptly filed suit against every other 3-D pub-

Two panels from Jack Davis's story "The Trophy," from *Three Dimensional Tales from the Crypt of Terror*

THE MONSTER FROM THE
FOURTH DIMENSION

I WAS IN THE SOUTH PASTURE OF MY FARM WHEN I FIRST SAW IT, HOVERING ABOUT TEN FEET OFF THE GROUND... AN OOZING, QUIVERING, RAW, FLESH-COVERED PULSATING MASS, GLIDING SLOWLY ACROSS THE FIELD...

AS IT MOVED, IT SEEMED TO GROW IN SIZE, ITS SHAPE CONSTANTLY CHANGING...

SUDDENLY, THE LIVID BLOB VANISHED AND I HEARD THE HOARSE WAIL OF AN ANIMAL SCREAMING IN PAIN...

lisher for infringement. The E.C. lawsuit drew a countersuit from St. John, and effectively enmeshed the 3-D comic business in a messy legal tangle.

Plodding calmly through it all, Gaines continued with preparations for his two comics. By the time they were finally published, in the spring of 1954, the luster had decidedly worn off 3-D. Both E.C. books were printed in small quantities—approximately 300,000—and both sold poorly.

The first, *Three-Dimensional E.C. Classics,* included stories by Wood, Krigstein, Evans, and Ingells, redrawn for 3-D from their original appearances in *Mad, Weird Science, Frontline Combat,* and *Crime SuspenStories. Classics* is an odd assemblage of the whacky and the mysterious, containing both a *Mad*-style story by Wallace Wood about a voluptuous vampiress—the only woman in all of 3-D who rated an extra plane for her bust—and an elegantly drawn Krigstein tale, "The Monster from the Fourth Dimension," in which deceptively simple graphics evoke the plain, open feeling of a Midwestern farm invaded by a gruesome time-traveling blob.

The second E.C. comic, *Three-Dimensional Tales from the Crypt of Terror,* is more consistently horrible. Stories by Davis, Elder, Craig, and Orlando have been redrawn from *Tales from the Crypt* and *The Vault of Horror,* to give the reader a chain of grisly 3-D thrills. Davis's contribution, "The Trophy," is a perennial fa-

Krigstein's "The Monster from the Fourth Dimension," from *Three Dimensional E.C. Classics,* employed unusually elegant graphics to tell an eerie story.

vorite in its flat version. Equally macabre are Elder's story, "The Strange Couple"—which at the end sends the reader spinning in an angst-producing cycle of repetition—Craig's piece about a true batman, and Orlando's "The Thing from the Grave."

All the stories in the second volume are introduced by the Crypt Keeper, E.C.'s famous M. C. of horror. He delights in serving up a nasty bill of severed heads, partly decayed corpses, and bloodthirsty fiends in a dank milieu, shaded to a heavy grayness by the E.C. artists.

The E.C. comics provided an appropriate finale to the brief flurry of 3-D comic publishing—a fitting last gasp. In April 1954 the national mood of suspicion about comic books provided Gaines with more serious worries than the failure of his two forays into 3-D. In that month he was called to testify in a special televised hearing before the U.S. Senate subcommittee investigating the causes of juvenile delinquency. Gaines's testimony followed that of Frederic Wertham, author of *Seduction of the Innocent*, and the senators were clearly eager to get political mileage out of grilling a horror-comic publisher. The *New York Times*, in a front-page story, described Senator Estes Kefauver asking Gaines if he considered in "good taste" the cover of one of his publications "which depicted an axe-wielding man holding aloft the severed head of a blonde woman." Gaines came off poorly in both the interrogation and the news accounts.

After his television appearance, sales of Gaines's comics plummeted, as newsdealers steered clear of the poisonous publicity. During the spring and summer more citizens' groups came out against comic books. The activists included the Women's Club Federation, the County and Prosecuting Attorney's Association, and the American Legion. In September 1954, comic-book publishers responded by forming the Comics Magazine Association to enforce a "comic code." As one of its first actions, the group banned crime and horror publications.

Comic books as a creative medium disappeared under this censorship, and the industry was not to recover for many years. William Gaines was forced to divest himself of every title except *Mad*, which he put into a longer, non-comic-book format, in order to sidestep the critical eye of the association. He is still saving the artwork he amassed for a 3-D science-fiction comic, completed in 1954 but never published because of the pressures of the marketplace. Someday, when he thinks the world is ready, Gaines will publish the book. With up to seven levels of depth, its art is more sophisticated than that in any 3-D comic book yet to appear.

And so 3-D comics, like 3-D movies, vanished as quickly as they had appeared. Unlike the movies, the comic books have not made even a sporadic return. A 1966 reprint of *3-D Batman* and a 1970 underground comic, *Deep 3-D Comix*, are all we have to show for almost thirty years of waiting. Most of the 3-D comics published during the heady days of 1953 and 1954 have long since been thrown away, and the few copies that have survived now command prices of twenty to seventy-five dollars—hundreds of times the original newsstand value.

E.C.'s 3-D glasses

OPPOSITE AND FOLLOWING PAGES: Will Elder's story "The Strange Couple," from *Three Dimensional Tales from the Crypt of Terror*

THE WOMAN POINTS TOWARD THE CELLAR DOOR.

MY *HUSBAND IS A VAMPIRE!* THAT IS WHY YOU MUST *LEAVE!* THAT *BOTTLE* HE'S BRINGING UP IS *ALMOST EMPTY!* IT'S *NOT WINE!* IT'S *BLOOD!*

GOOD LORD THIS WO... IS MAD

THE FOOTSTEPS ON THE CELLAR STAIRS WARN THE OLD WOMAN OF HER HUSBAND'S RETURN, AND AS SHE SCURRIES INTO THE SHADOWS OF THE FIREPLACE...

AH! *HERE* WE ARE!

THE MAN PUTS THE BOTTLE ON THE TABLE, AND YOU STARE AT IT. IT *IS* ALMOST EMPTY... AND ITS CONTENTS ARE A DEEP RED... *BLOOD RED...*

YOU'LL *JOIN* ME, SIR!

I'D... I'D *RATHER*

HE JUMPS UP ANGRILY. HE RUSHES TO THE WOMAN...

YOU'VE BEEN *TALKING!* GO TO YOUR ROOM! *GO AHEAD!*

Y-YES, FEDOR!

THE MAN RETURNS TO THE TABLE. YOU CAN SEE THAT HE IS IRRITATED. HE POURS HIMSELF A GLASS OF RED LIQUID AND DRINKS IT DOWN, LICKING HIS LIPS. THEN HE LEANS TOWARD YOU...

YOU MUSTN'T LISTEN TO HER. SHE'S A...*GHOUL!!* INSANE...HELPLESSLY INSANE. MY WIFE IS...A *GHOUL!*

ICY FINGERS CLOSE AROUND YOUR HEART AS THE MAN RELATES A STRANGE TALE...

WE HAD A *DOG!* ONE DAY, IT *DIED.* I BURIED THE POOR THING IN THE GARDEN. THAT NIGHT, I WAS AWAKENED BY THE SOUND OF *DIGGING.* I LOOKED OUT OF THE WINDOW!

150

YOU LOOK AROUND...

THAT *BUREAU* LOOKS HEAVY ENOUGH!

YOU PUSH THE HEAVY BUREAU UP AGAINST THE DOOR TO HIS ROOM...

THAT OUGHT TO DO IT! HE CAN'T MOVE *THAT!*

THEN YOU LOCK THE CLOSET WITH THE KEY THAT THE MAN HAS GIVEN YOU...

THERE MAY BE ANOTHER KEY TO THE *CLOSET,* TOO!

YOU MOVE THE HEAVY IRON BED UP AGAINST THE CLOSET DOOR...

IF *I LIE* ON THE BED, SHE WON'T BE ABLE TO *PUSH IT OPEN!*

YOU STRETCH OUT ON THE BED, LISTENING TO THE RAIN POUNDING ON THE ROOF ABOVE...

WHO...WHO CAN I *BELIEVE?* WHICH ONE IS TELLING THE *TRUTH?* OR IS THIS ALL SOME *HORRIBLE JOKE!*

SUDDENLY, YOU SIT BOLT-UPRIGHT! A NOISE...OUTSIDE YOUR ROOM...IN THE HALL. FOOTSTEPS! YOUR BLOOD FREEZES...

THE...THE *MAN?* IS HE *OUT THERE?*

SUDDENLY YOU OPEN YOUR EYES. THE LIGHTNING FLASHES...

GOOD LORD!

YOU ARE IN A CAR, THE RAIN POUNDING ON THE METAL TOP, ECHOING IN YOUR BRAIN. YOU'RE WET WITH PERSPIRATION, AND *SICK*...

I... I MUST HAVE BEEN *DREAMING!*

YOU SETTLE BACK, RESIGNED TO WAITING UNTIL THE STORM ABATES, WHEN SUDDENLY, YOU SEE A LIGHT... SHINING THROUGH THE BLACK DOWNPOUR...

A *FARM-HOUSE!* PERHAPS THEY HAVE A *PHONE!*

YOU PULL YOUR COLLAR UP AROUND YOUR NECK, PULL YOUR HAT DOWN, AND BREAK FOR THE HOUSE...

IF THEY HAVE NO *PHONE*, PERHAPS THEY CAN *PUT ME UP FOR THE NIGHT.*

THE HOUSE IS OLD AND RUN DOWN. THE SHUTTERS ARE BROKEN AND CLATTER AGAINST THE WINDOWS. ICY FINGERS GRIP YOUR SPINE. YOUR *NIGHTMARE! IT'S JUST LIKE THE HOUSE IN YOUR NIGHTMARE!*

BAH! IT WAS ONLY A DREAM!

YOU KNOCK. THE HOLLOW BOOM ECHOES THROUGH THE INTERIOR. HEAVY FOOTSTEPS APPROACH. THE DOOR SWINGS OPEN ON RUSTY STRAINING HINGES...

GO AWAY! GO *AWAY* FROM HERE BEFORE IT'S TOO *LATE!*

LET THE GENTLEMAN COME IN, HEPSIBAH!

ONLY A DREAM? WELL? THEN WHAT ARE YOU *FRIGHTENED* OF? GO ON! *GO ON IN!*

THE END

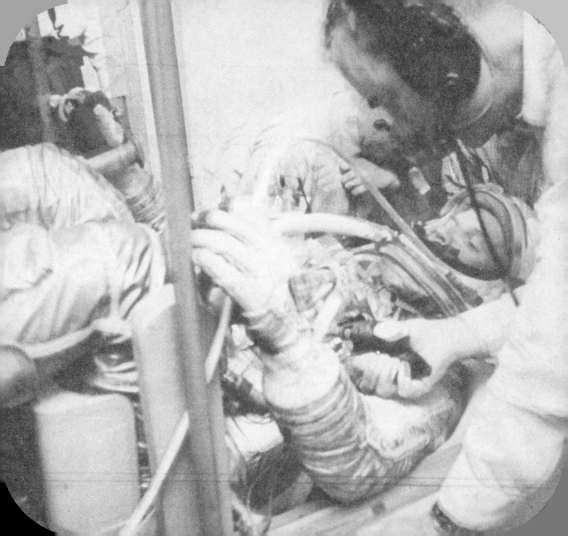

5.

THE BIG SLEEP

3-D Since 1955

Reviewing the progress of 3-D since the 1950s is a little like going to a thirtieth high school reunion. Some of the brightest stars of 1953 and 1954 have faded into nothing, and some others, which were hardly noticed then, have grown into the best hopes for the future.

Stereo photography did not die as suddenly or as profoundly as the 3-D movies and comic books and, by comparison, has been thriving in a low-key way. Unlike movies or comic books, cameras are bought to be kept and used. Many of the hundreds of thousands of stereo cameras sold in the 1950s are still in active use, generating enough business to warrant Kodak continuing its mounting service.

The Stereo Realist toughed it out through the 1960s, until its production line finally closed down in 1971. It even had some fresh competition in its last years, when the View-Master Mark II appeared from Sawyer's Belgium in 1962. The Mark II used a diagonal film path to take stereo View-Master slides on 35-mm film, and it sold in the United States for only $78.50, about half the price of its predecessor, the View-Master Personal.

The View-Master reels and viewers have been plugging along toward their fifty-year mark with steady sales. After some rocky times under the ownership of GAF—from 1967 to 1981—the company is now poised for a resurgence, with new owners and an ambitious new president. Current reel lists include old favorites and exciting new offerings, like *Kiss*—ablaze with incredible 3-D lighting effects—and a new series of baseball reels. The Talking View-Master, which combines the picture disks with miniature records, is being redesigned in Japan and should soon be available in an improved, compact version. The company has released commemorative viewers for special occasions, most recently a royal purple model sold only in England to mark the wedding of Prince Charles to Lady Diana. The product improvements at View-Master are being matched with new promotion efforts—full-page advertisements in national magazines and flashy store

OPPOSITE PAGE: John Glenn undergoes a medical examination in full dress before his historic orbital space flight. RIGHT: A model of the flight. Both photographs are from the 1962 View-Master reel set, *America's Man in Space*.

display units—that should serve to send the system soaring once again.

Other 3-D viewing systems have appeared occasionally. One of these is Big Bird's 3-D camera, which holds a Sesame Street film loop. And in other countries various other systems have enjoyed long and healthy lives. The French Brugiére Stéréocartes hold eight high-quality stereo transparencies on rectangular cards similar to the old Tru-Vue cards. They have been made since the 1950s by Stéréofilms Brugiére and are still sold in this country by the Milwaukee Stereo Exchange (Box 1186, Milwaukee, Wisconsin 53211). Disk systems like View-Master's, but with slightly different formats, exist in Italy and East Germany.

In 1975 a new stereo camera came out—the all-plastic Stereo 35, made by Meopta of Czechoslovakia. Like the View-Master Mark II, the Stereo 35 took View-Master-format pictures on 35-mm film using a diagonal film path. In the spring of 1982 the Nimslo camera was introduced, a major new presence in 3-D, designed for making lenticular 3-D photographic prints. The Nimslo has four lenses for taking four side-by-side images. In the processing the images are merged into extremely narrow strips behind a ridged lenticular screen. The result is a finely detailed, full-color, three-dimensional print viewable without optical aids or glasses.

The Nimslo was designed by Jerry Nims and Allen Lo and refined with the help of engineers at Timex.

Sesame Street's Big Bird 3-D viewer, shaped like a camera, holds an alphabet stereo film strip.

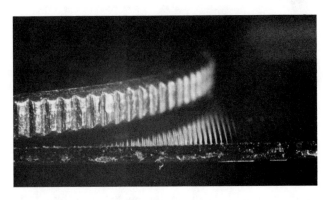

The surface of the Nimslo print is a finely ridged lenticular screen, compared here with the edge of a dime.

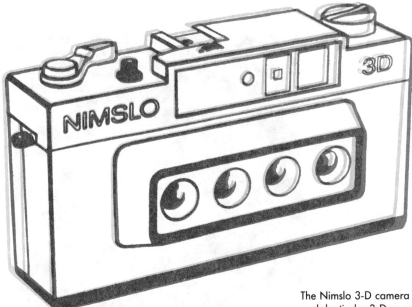

The Nimslo 3-D camera takes four simultaneous pictures for each lenticular 3-D snapshot.

The camera is being manufactured in Scotland at a facility large enough to produce 450,000 cameras a year in a single shift—enough to outnumber all existing stereo cameras by the end of 1982. The price of the camera is roughly two hundred dollars, depending on the place of purchase, and the prints are only slightly more expensive than normal color photographs—about seventy-five cents each. The Nimslo is certain to revive public interest in 3-D photography. Perhaps it will become the Stereo Realist of the 1980s.

Anaglyphic (two-color 3-D) printing has no such dynamic future in store. The comic books and movie-fan magazines of 1953 and 1954 were clearly the anaglyphs' finest hour.

Though little effort has gone into creating better 3-D artwork, the design of 3-D glasses has advanced dramatically. A 1966 reissue of D.C.'s *3-D Batman* comic book included a wild pair of bat glasses, which could have sold alone for the price of the comic book. D.C.'s bat designer may have been inspired by the anaglyphic glasses made for the 1961 horror film *The Mask*, which were made to transform audiences into voodoo demons.

Deep 3-D Comix, the only underground comic to go 3-D, was published in 1970 by Krupp Comic Works, the makers of *Bijou Funnies*. Appropriately, the glasses included in that book had round porthole windows and were covered with a pattern of bubbles (Deep 3-D; get it?). Instead of the usual 1953 endorsement

Modern anaglyphic 3-D glasses. From top: glasses from the 1961 film *The Mask*; glasses from the 1966 reissue of National's 3-D Batman comic book; glasses from *Deep 3-D Comix*, the only 3-D underground comic book.

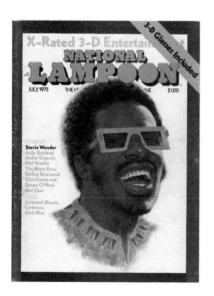

The cover of the July 1975 3-D issue of the *National Lampoon*.

of 3-D by "a noted New York eye specialist" Krupp put in a more unusual disclaimer: "It is a *malicious lie* that 3-D glasses cause kids to go blind. Researchers at Parson's College found that *less than 10%* of children so observed went totally blind, and *nearly half* suffered *absolutely no* eye damage at all!" Inside, readers were treated to news of a new TV game show called "Shuck Your Mother," saw President Nixon's head inflated with a pump for a public appearance, and read about a computer that defected to join "the underground."

Safely on this side of the 1960s, the *National Lampoon* put out a 3-D issue in July 1975. The cover—marking the absolute nadir of 3-D taste—showed Stevie Wonder wearing a pair of the red and blue glasses. Eye-wrenching 3-D ads for audio equipment

The final panel of the Gahan Wilson cartoon "Nuts," from the 1975 3-D issue of the *National Lampoon*

pepper the inside, along with deepened versions of *Lampoon* regulars Dirty Duck and Thelma Ironthighs. A good Gahan Wilson cartoon, "Nuts," makes up for much of the cruder work in the magazine.

American Cinematographer, Starlog, Australian Playboy, Club, and *Swank* have all published anaglyph issues in recent years, and some nifty 3-D promotional items have also appeared. In 1978 7-Eleven convenience stores distributed a series of historic American views, with a pair of folding glasses, all in a compact package; and McDonald's, in 1981, sold a boxed children's meal, called a "3-D Happy Meal," at selected locations. The McDonald's box has anaglyph render-

ings of old stereo views and a modern cartoon on the outside. Children look at the 3-D effect through a pair of glasses shaped like the golden arches.

3-D movies, smothered by the competition, CinemaScope, lay dormant for years after *Revenge of the Creature.* But, as we all know, you can't keep a good thing down. Stereophonic sound systems became commonplace during the 1960s and 1970s, and stereoscopic movies just kept trying.

The first sign of life came in 1960, with the release of *September Storm,* a two-strip Cinemascope 3-D picture from 20th Century-Fox. Technical problems with projection and an inferior script limited its 3-D release somewhat. A short, *Charito and Ernesto,* and a cartoon, *Space Attack,* were also on the bill. At about the same time a skin flick titled *Adam and Six Eves* was made, anticipating a trend in 3-D movies. (The 1960 William Castle production *13 Ghosts* was *not* 3-D, though many people believe it was. Certain sequences required the use of a viewer with orange and blue filters, but only to see the film's "ghosts." The viewer was made so that both eyes looked through the same colored filter.)

The following year Warner's released the thriller *The Mask.* Produced by Toronto-based Taylor-Roffman Productions, it featured three five-minute anaglyphic segments. It is regarded as one of the best anaglyphic film presentations ever.

In 1962 a partially 3-D skin flick, *Bellboy and the Play-*

McDonald's "3-D Happy Meal"

A still from *The Mask*

girls, popped up (or out). The 3-D portion—the last seventeen minutes—was available to theaters for anaglyphic or polarized projection. Far from being a great film, *Bellboy* did feature the debut of a promising young director—Francis Ford Coppola. The same year Jack Harris's *Paradisio* was released; the sections in anaglyphic 3-D were as bad as the story line. With that, 3-D film again disappeared for another four years of rest and recuperation.

On December 21, 1966, a movie featuring a "new" screen process premiered in Chicago. The process was "4-D Space-Vision," the picture was *The Bubble,* and the producer was Arch Oboler. Technically, Oboler's second 3-D film was vastly superior to his first. The process, which was developed by Robert Bernier (patent no. 3,531,191), was the first commercially practical "stacked" system—wherein pairs of stereo images, each a full 35-mm frame, are stacked one above the other on the strip of film. Such systems had begun to be used for 3-D projection in 1954, but had not gained wide acceptance.

The Bubble, which brought newcomer Michael Cole to the big screen, was much too long. Audiences, impressed by the sophisticated 3-D process and the new, comfortable glasses, were bored by the 112-minute film, which should have been cut to about 30 minutes. Financially *The Bubble* was a bust. In 1976 a new distri-

An advertisement for *Fantastic Invasion of the Planet Earth,* the new name for Arch Oboler's 1966 film, *The Bubble*

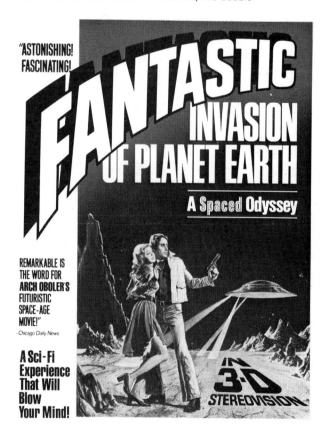

butor, Monarch Leasing, retitled it *Fantastic Invasion of the Planet Earth,* and it has since fared a little better.

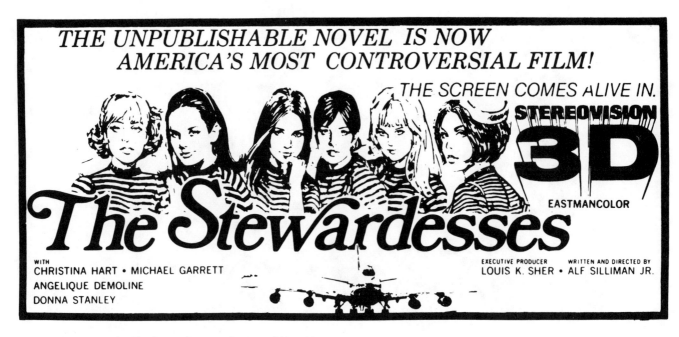

An advertisement for *The Stewardesses,* at the time of this writing the highest grossing 3-D film ever made

Sometime in 1968 three collaborators decided to make a short 3-D girlie flick. Using an Eyemo and an old Wall 35-mm camera fitted with special prisms, they produced enough footage to release their work under the now-famous title, *The Stewardesses.* Test runs in San Francisco and Los Angeles made one thing quite apparent: people were very eager to see X-rated 3-D, regardless of its quality.

More than half the film was reshot using improved optics and talent. The result is a ninety-eight-minute feature, that, for an approximate cost of $100,000, made $26 million at the box office and ushered in a new wave of 3-D, the largest since 1953.

Trying to cash in on the 3-D excitement, a small outfit in New York threw one of the most abominable films at an unsuspecting public—*Swing Tail.* Presented in an approximated anaglyphic form, the colors on the screen (blue and purplish magenta) in no way matched the red and green glasses. In 1972 another amateurish attempt was released: the German-made *Frankenstein's Bloody Terror,* shown with plastic projection components that completely destroyed any quality the film might have had. It was rapidly removed from release after box-office returns indicated something short of success.

StereoVision International (by this time of *Stewardesses* fame) purchased the release rights from War-

ner's for the classic *House of Wax* and had it printed in Technicolor in a 70-mm single-strip, side-by-side format. A few trial engagements in Ohio during October 1971 proved the merit of the idea, and led to a "premiere" at Grauman's Chinese Theater in Hollywood, on November 16. It was the first time a 3-D film or a reissue had played at the theater, and it did quite well. Local elementary schools sent classes to the presentation as an educational field trip.

In December 1971, United Producers ran a test engagement of *The Secrets of Ecstasy '72* in Boston and several other cities, but projection problems caused the venture to be abandoned. *The Three Dimensions of Greta,* from England, had four short anaglyphic segments, which in most scenes were misaligned, causing considerable eyestrain. United Producers returned in 1972 with *Prison Girls.* Poorly written, directed, and photographed, the movie is one of the most blatant examples of the damaging misuse of the 3-D film medium.

Other disappointments of recent years include *Ram Rod, The Playmates, International Stewardesses,* and *Funk in 3-D.* Not quite so bad, but not quality films, either, are the German *Lieben 3-D (Love in 3-D)* and the Swedish *A Man With a Maid* (renamed *The Groove Room*).

Arch Oboler's third 3-D effort, *Domo Arigato (Thank*

160

You Very Much), was also his best, but it played on a limited test basis in Los Angeles and Seattle only. Filmed in Japan, it is a fascinating and somewhat entertaining travelog featuring the beautiful scenery of Japan.

Andy Warhol's Frankenstein, originally called *Flesh for Frankenstein*, was successfully released in 1974 and has become 3-D's second biggest grosser to date, just behind *The Stewardesses*. Starring Joe Dallesandro, Udo Kier, and Monique Van Vooren, the film parodies the horror genre. Liberal doses of violence and sex earned it an X rating when it first appeared, since modified to an R.

New York filmmaker Mike Findlay, after a dismal first try with *Funk in 3-D,* went to Taiwan in 1976 and filmed a Kung-Fu epic titled *Dynasty,* followed immediately by *13 Nuns.* Both have serious technical flaws, and of the two only *Dynasty* has managed even a limited release in the United States. That same year a low-budget 3-D remake of *King Kong* was filmed in Korea, released with the title *A*P*E.*

Porno entries dominated the next few years, with *Surfer Girls, Man Hole, Heavy Equipment, The Capitol Hill Girls, Wildcat Women,* and *Lollipop Girls in Hard Candy. The Starlets* was a technically superior effort—in full-color polarized 3-D—and *Experiments in Love* was an interesting film in which the actresses play experimental 3-D filmmakers.

General audiences were largely neglected by 3-D in the late 1970s. Two films from China received limited distribution; these were *The North and South Chivalry* in 1978, and *The Magnificent Bodyguards* in 1979. Theaters like the Tiffany in Hollywood, the Avenue in San Francisco, the Thalia and the 8th Street Playhouse

Advertisements for a few of the 3-D films from the 1970s. From top to bottom: *Andy Warhol's Frankenstein, The Capital Hill Girls, The Starlets,* and *Experiments in Love.* The fourth D claimed for the last two films was, according to the promotional literature, the dimension of "sensual involvement."

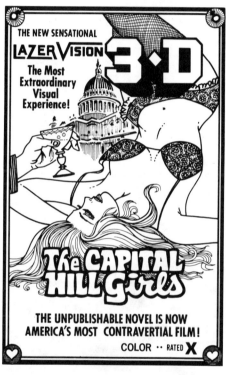

in New York, and Coolidge Corner in Boston began reviving the 3-D classics from the 1950s for a growing cult following. But not until 1981, with *Comin' at Ya!*, was there a major new release.

Comin' at Ya! was produced by a trio of movie novices: Gene Quintano and Marshall Lupo—both former Xerox salesmen—and actor Tony Anthony. Directed by Italian Ferdinando Baldi, the film runs along more like a 3-D demonstration than a narrative movie. Every three minutes something is thrown at or dumped on the audience: beans, bats, arrows, even a baby partway through a diaper change. But the film did well for its investors, grossing over eight million dollars before the end of its first year. Quintano, Lupo,

and Anthony are busily at work on a second 3-D feature, to be called *Seein' Is Believin'*, which is scheduled for a summer 1982 release.

3-D movie fans can look forward to some exciting days just ahead. 1982 releases include *Parasite* (released March 1982), *Bayou*, *Rottweiler*, and *Surf!!*—a musical comedy starring Linda Kerridge and Bo Derek's lovely sister, Kelly Collins. *House of Wax* and *Dial M For Murder* are being re-released nationally with new advertising and publicity campaigns. And a stunning new 3-D film, *Sea Dream*, is now thrilling audiences at Marineland in Florida. Its creator, Murray Lerner, is preparing another 3-D feature, sponsored by Kodak, to be shown at Disney World.

A promotional display for *Rottweiler*

THE
MOST EXCITING
AND TERRIFYING 3-DIMENSIONAL FILM
YOU WILL EVER SEE!

STARRING
TEN OF THE DEADLIEST DOGS
IN THE WORLD!

The creature from the black lagoon makes a thrilling appearance on 3-D television. This photograph was created by 3-D Video, the company that has engineered the revival of 3-D on television.

Television holds even more promise for the revival of 3-D. SelecTV, a cable station in Los Angeles, aired *Miss Sadie Thompson* and the Three Stooges short *Spooks* on December 19, 1980 in the first of what has grown to be a flurry of 3-D television broadcasts. Every subscriber got a coupon, redeemable for two pairs of anaglyphic glasses at local Sears stores, with his program guide. The broadcast was hugely successful, and SelecTV has since treated its subscribers to a number of other 3-D films, including *Bwana Devil*, *House of Wax*, *The Mad Magician*, and *Andy Warhol's Frankenstein*.

3-D Video Corporation is the source of the technology that made these broadcasts possible. Its president, James Butterfield, devised the 3-D Video System of converting the films into a form suitable for television broadcast. The company has engineered 3-D cable broadcasts in cities throughout the country, and has made 3-D films accessible to distributors of video cassettes and disks.

The next big step, the first over-the-air 3-D broadcast on commercial television, came in New Orleans on February 9, 1982, when station WGNO showed *Revenge of the Creature.* Two days before the broadcast three hundred thousand pairs of glasses had been sold through an arrangement with local Timesaver stores, and Nielsen reported that an astounding forty percent of all viewers watched the show.

We can expect to see much more 3-D television in the future as new and better 3-D films are made and as programs are prepared specially for 3-D broadcast. In April and May 1982, forty-six stations throughout the United States broadcast in 3-D. So save the glasses that came with this book. The filters are the right colors for viewing 3-D TV.

The next great frontier for the improvement of 3-D seems to lie in holography, which over the last several years has made great strides toward commercial practicality. Large display holographs can now be made that require only the illumination of white light to create the illusion of a solid object in space. Moving holograms are also being made—though so far their duration is limited to less than a minute.

The principles of holography were first described by Dennis Gabor in 1948, well before there was a suitable light source to realize the images. In 1960 the first laser was produced, bringing a practical source of coherent light—light in which the waves are of the same length and are synchronized across their width to the same wave pattern. Using laser light, scientists Emmet Leith and Juris Upatnieks of the University of Michigan produced the first holograms.

Stephen A. Benton, of the Polaroid Research Laboratories, with "The Rind," a white light transmission hologram. The latest generation of holograms can be displayed in full three dimensions with the illumination of an ordinary incandescent light bulb.

Basically a hologram is formed by an interference pattern of light waves coming to the holographic plate from two directions. Laser light is split into two paths—one reflected off the object to be recorded, the other crossing the reflected light at an angle. The interference pattern created by the crossing beams is recorded at the surface of the holographic plate. By recreating the action of the second beam of light—shining it on the developed holographic plate at the same angle as the original beam during exposure—the object half of the interference pattern is distilled, and a three-dimensional image of the object is formed.

Thanks to the patient efforts of researchers like Stephen Benton at the Polaroid Corporation, Lloyd Cross, and Richard Rallinson, holograms need no longer be viewed with laser light. The remarkable state of holographic science and art can be seen in traveling holography exhibitions, or at the Museum of Holography in New York City (11 Mercer Street, in Soho, zip 10012). Holograms are already used as three-dimensional cataloguing tools at museums, as illustrations in books, and even as jewelry. It now seems only a matter of time before holography researchers surmount the remaining problems of color, motion, and projection.

The future looks bright for 3-D. We have 3-D pictures of Mars—even though no man has ever set foot there—and, with them, by seeing in depth that unreachable landscape, we have evidence of the powerful reality contained in 3-D images.

We have a new 3-D camera for taking snapshots with depth, a slew of new 3-D movies to choose from, and 3-D on our home televisions. We are facing the future with both eyes open, and the depths and delights ahead seem infinite.

Chronology of Three-Dimensional Motion Pictures

Before 1950

FILM TITLE	DATE	PRODUCER	SYSTEM
The Power of Love	1922	Fairall	Anaglyphic
Movies of the Future	1922	Kelley	Anaglyphic
M.A.R.S.	1922	Hammond and Cassidy	Teleview
Plastigrams	1924	Educational Pictures/Ives and Leventhal	Anaglyphic
A Runaway Taxi	1925	Pathe/Ives and Leventhal	Anaglyphic
Ouch	1925	Pathe/Ives and Leventhal	Anaglyphic
Zowie	1925	Pathe/Ives and Leventhal	Anaglyphic
Lunacy	1925	Pathe/Ives and Leventhal	Anaglyphic
Nozze Vagabond (Italian)	1936		Polarized
Audioscopiks	1936	MGM/Smith, Norling, and Leventhal	Anaglyphic
Zum Greifen Nah (German)	1937		Polarized
New Audioscopiks	1938	MGM/Smith, Norling, and Leventhal	Anaglyphic
In Tune With Tomorrow	1939	Chrysler/Polaroid/Norling	Polarized
Six Girls Drive into the Weekend (German)	1939		Polarized
Day Off in Moscow (Russian)	1940		Lenticular
Concerto (Russian)	1941		Lenticular
Third Dimension Murder	1941	MGM/Smith	Anaglyphic
Robinson Crusoe (Russian)	1947		Lenticular
Queen Juliana (Dutch)	1948		Polarized
Aleko (Russian)	1948?		Lenticular
In the Steppes (Russian)	1948?		Lenticular
Lalim (Russian)	?		Lenticular
May Night (Russian)	?		Lenticular
Pal (Russian)	?		Lenticular
Precious Gift (Russian)	?		Lenticular

1950 to 1959, Features

FILM TITLE	DATE	PRODUCER	SYSTEM
Wintertime Tale (Hungarian)	1952?		Polarized
Bwana Devil	1952	Oboler/United Artists	Polarized
Man in the Dark	1953	Columbia	Polarized
House of Wax	1953	Warner Bros.	Polarized
It Came from Outer Space	1953	Universal	Polarized
Fort Ti	1953	Columbia	Polarized
Sangaree	1953	Paramount	Polarized

FILM TITLE	DATE	PRODUCER	SYSTEM
Arena	1953	MGM	Polarized
Robot Monster	1953	Astor	Polarized
The Maze	1953	Allied Artists	Polarized
Charge at Feather River	1953	Warner Bros.	Polarized
Hannah Lee (renamed Outlaw Territory)	1953	Realart	Polarized
Second Chance	1953	RKO	Polarized
Inferno	1953	20th Century-Fox	Polarized
I, the Jury	1953	United Artists	Polarized
The Stranger Wore a Gun	1953	Columbia	Polarized
Devil's Canyon	1953	RKO	Polarized
Wings of the Hawk	1953	Universal	Polarized
The Moonlighter	1953	Warner Bros.	Polarized
Those Redheads from Seattle	1953	Paramount	Polarized
Flight to Tangier	1953	Paramount	Polarized
The Glass Web	1953	Universal	Polarized
Kiss Me Kate	1953	MGM	Polarized
Gun Fury	1953	Columbia	Polarized
The Nebraskan	1953	Columbia	Polarized
Louisiana Territory	1953	RKO	Polarized
Hondo	1953	Warner Bros./Wayne-Fellows	Polarized
Cease Fire	1953	Paramount/Wallis	Polarized
Miss Sadie Thompson	1953	Columbia	Polarized
Cat Women of the Moon	1953	Astor	Polarized
Beauty to Measure (Italian)	1953		Polarized
El Corazon y la Espada (Mexican)	1953	Azteca	Anaglyphic
The Fortune Hunters (Japanese)	1953		Polarized
Tailor-Made Beauties (Italian)	1953		Polarized
Drums of Tahiti	1954	Columbia	Polarized
Taza, Son of Cochise	1954	Universal	Polarized
Creature from the Black Lagoon	1954	Universal	Polarized
Money from Home	1954	Paramount	Polarized
The French Line	1954	RKO	Polarized
Phantom of the Rue Morgue	1954	Warner Bros.	Polarized
Jesse James vs the Daltons	1954	Columbia	Polarized
Dangerous Mission	1954	RKO	Polarized
Jivaro	1954	Paramount	Polarized
The Mad Magician	1954	Columbia	Polarized
Southwest Passage	1954	United Artists	Polarized
Dial M for Murder	1954	Warner Bros.	Polarized
Gorilla at Large	1954	20th Century-Fox	Polarized
Son of Sinbad	1954	RKO	Polarized
Gog	1954	United Artists	Polarized
Crystal (Russian)	1954		Lenticular
Machine 22-12 (Russian)	1954		Lenticular

1950 to 1959, Features, continued

FILM TITLE	DATE	PRODUCER	SYSTEM
The Pencil on Ice (Russian)	1954?		Lenticular
Silver Lode	1954	United Artists	Polarized
Revenge of the Creature	1955	Universal	Polarized

1950 to 1959, Shorts and cartoons

Around Is Around (British)	1951	Spottiswoodes	Polarized
The Black Swan (British)	1951	Spottiswoodes	Polarized
A Solid Explanation (British)	1951	Spottiswoodes	Polarized
Royal River (British)	1951		Polarized
Now Is the Time (Canadian)	1951	McLaren	Polarized
Artist's Examination (Hungarian)	1952		Polarized
Capstan Cigarettes (British)	1952		Polarized
May Day 1952 (Hungarian)	1952		Polarized
3-D Musical	1952		Polarized
Time for Beanie (prologue to *Bwana Devil*)	1952	Gunzburg/United Artists	Polarized
Melody	1953	Disney	Polarized
Nat "King" Cole Sings "Pretend"	1953	Universal	Polarized
Spooks	1953	Columbia	Polarized
Pardon My Backfire	1953	"	Polarized
Hypnotic Hick	1953	Universal/Lantz	Polarized
Boo Moon	1953	Paramount	Polarized
Lumberjack Rabbit	1953	Warner Bros.	Polarized
Popeye, Ace of Space	1953	Paramount	Polarized
Working for Peanuts	1953	Disney	Polarized
Marciano-Walcott Fight	1953	Lippert	Polarized
Bandit Island	1953	Lippert	Polarized
Assignment A-Bomb	1953		Polarized
Carnival in April	1953	Universal	Polarized
College Capers (British)	1953		Polarized
Coronation of Queen Elizabeth (British)	1953		Polarized
A Day in the Country (British)	1953		Polarized
Doom Town	1953		Polarized
I Am Marked (Japanese)	1953		Polarized
Jumping Out Sunday (Japanese)	1953		Polarized
London Tribute (British)	1953		Polarized
Milwaukee-Chicago Baseball Game	1953		Polarized
Motor Rhythm	1953	RKO	Polarized
The Owl and the Pussycat	1953		Polarized
Royal Flush (British)	1953	Lippert	Polarized
Side Streets of Hollywood	1953		Anaglyphic
Star of the Screen (Dutch)	1953		Polarized
Tell-Tale Heart (British)	1953	Columbia	Polarized

1950 to 1959, Shorts and cartoons, continued

FILM TITLE	DATE	PRODUCER	SYSTEM
This is Triorama	1953		Polarized
3-D Follies	1953		Polarized
Volkswagen (German)	1953		Polarized
A Way of Thinking (shown in Mobile Theater)	1954	Ramsdell	Polarized

1960 to 1982, Features

September Storm	1960	20th Century-Fox	Polarized
Adam and Six Eves	1960		Polarized
The Mask	1961	Warner Bros./Beaver-Champion	Anaglyphic (partial)
The Bellboy and the Playgirls	1962	United Producers	Polarized/Anaglyphic
Paradisio	1962	Harris	Anaglyphic (partial)
The Bubble (renamed Fantastic Invasion of the Planet Earth)	1966	Oboler	Polarized
The Stewardesses	1969	Stereovision	Polarized
Swing Tail	1971		Anaglyphic (partial)
Secrets of Ecstasy '72	1972	United Producers	Polarized
Three Dimensions of Greta (British)	1972		Anaglyphic (partial)
Prison Girls	1972	United Producers	Polarized
The Chamber Maids	1972		Polarized
Frankenstein's Bloody Terror (German)	1972		Polarized
Lieben 3-D (German; released in U.S. as Love in 3-D)	1972		Polarized
A Man and a Maid (Swedish; renamed The Groove Room and What the Swedish Butler Saw)	1973	Victorian/Becker	Polarized
Domo Arigato	1973	Oboler	Polarized
Asylum of the Insane	1973		Anaglyphic (partial)
The Playmates	1973	Gibson	Anaglyphic
Ram Rod	1973		Polarized
International Stewardesses	1973	Stereovision	Polarized
Andy Warhol's Frankenstein	1974	Ponti, Braunsberg, and Rossam	Polarized
Funk in 3-D	1975	Findlay	Polarized
Capital Hill Girls	1975	Stereovision	Polarized
Manhole	1975	Marks	Polarized
A*P*E	1976		Polarized
Dynasty	1976	Findlay	Polarized
Lollipop Girls in Hard Candy	1976	Gibson	Anaglyphic
The Starlets	1976	Alpha	Polarized
Experiments in Love	1976	Alpha	Polarized
Surfer Girls	1976	Stereovision	Polarized
13 Nuns (renamed Revenge of the Shogun Women)	1976	Findlay	Polarized
Heavy Equipment	1977		Anaglyphic
Wildcat Women	1977	Gibson	Anaglyphic

1960 to 1982, Features, continued

FILM TITLE	DATE	PRODUCER	SYSTEM
The North and South Chivalry (Chinese)	1978		Polarized
Sea Dream	1978	Marineland	Polarized
The Magnificent Bodyguards (Chinese)	1979		Polarized
Comin' At Ya	1981	Lupo, Anthony, and Quintano	Polarized
Parasite	1982	Embassy	Polarized

1960 to 1982, Shorts and cartoons

Charito and Ernesto	1960	20th Century-Fox	Polarized
Space Attack	1960	20th Century-Fox	Polarized
Two Guys from Tick Ridge	1973	United Producers	Polarized

Chronology of Three-Dimensional Comic Books

TITLE	ISSUE	DATE	PUBLISHER
Three Dimension Comics (Mighty Mouse)	no. 1	Sept. 1953	St. John Publishing Co.
Three Dimension Comics (Mighty Mouse reprint)	no. 1	Oct. 1953	St. John Publishing Co.
3-D Comics (Tor)	no. 2	Oct. 1953	St. John Publishing Co.
Three Stooges	no. 2	Oct. 1953	St. John Publishing Co.
Whack	no. 1	Oct. 1953	St. John Publishing Co.
House of Terror	no. 1	Oct. 1953	St. John Publishing Co.
Little Eva	no. 1	Oct. 1953	St. John Publishing Co.
3-D-ell (Rootie Kazootie)	no. 1	Oct. 1953	Dell Publishing Co.
Three Dimension Comics (Mighty Mouse)	no. 2	Nov. 1953	St. John Publishing Co.
3-D Comics (Tor)	no. 2	Nov. 1953	St. John Publishing Co.
Three Stooges	no. 3	Nov. 1953	St. John Publishing Co.
The Hawk	no. 1	Nov. 1953	St. John Publishing Co.
Abbott and Costello	no. 1	Nov. 1953	St. John Publishing Co.
Daring Adventures	no. 1	Nov. 1953	St. John Publishing Co.
Adventures in 3-D	no. 1	Nov. 1953	Harvey Publications
Superman in Startling 3-D Life-Like Action		Nov. 1953	National Comics Publications
3-D-ell (Rootie Kazootie)	no. 2	Nov. 1953	Dell Publishing Co.
Three Dimension Comics (Mighty Mouse)	no. 3	Dec. 1953	St. John Publishing Co.
True 3-D	no. 1	Dec. 1953	Harvey Publications
Captain 3-D	no. 1	Dec. 1953	Home Comics
Funny 3-D	no. 1	Dec. 1953	Harvey Publications
3-D Dolly	no. 1	Dec. 1953	Harvey Features Syndicate
3-D-ell (Flukey Luke)	no. 3	Dec. 1953	Dell Publishing Co.
3-D Sheena the Jungle Queen	no. 1	Dec. 1953	Real Adventures Publishing Co.
The First Christmas		Dec. 1953	Real Adventures Publishing Co.
3-D Circus	no. 1	Dec. 1953	Real Adventures Publishing Co.
3-D Love	no. 1	Dec. 1953	Steriographic Publications
Katy Keene Three Dimension Comics	no. 1	Dec. 1953	Close-Up, Inc.
Felix the Cat 3-D Comic Book	no. 1	Dec. 1953	Toby Press
Batman Adventures in Amazing 3-D Action		Dec. 1953	National Periodical Publications
Animal Fun 3-D	no. 1	Dec. 1953	Premier Magazines
3-D Funny Movies	no. 1	Dec. 1953	Allen Hardy Associates
Indian Warriors	no. 1	Dec. 1953	Star Publications

TITLE	ISSUE	DATE	PUBLISHER
Jungle Thrills	no. 1	Dec. 1953	Star Publications
Western Fighters	no. 1	Dec. 1953	Star Publications
Jet Pup	no. 1	Dec. 1953	Dimensions Publications
Noodnick	no. 1	Dec. 1953	Harwell Publications
The Space Kat-Ets	no. 1	Dec. 1953	Power Publishing Co.
Super Animals	no. 1	Dec. 1953	Star Publications
Super Funnies	no. 1	Dec. 1953	Superior Publishers
Adventures in 3-D	no. 2	Jan. 1954	Harvey Publications
Harvey 3-D Hits (Sad Sack)	no. 1	Jan. 1954	Harvey 3-D Hits
Jiggs and Maggie	no. 26	Jan. 1954	Harvey Publications
Katzenjammer Kids	no. 26	Jan. 1954	Harvey Publications
3-D Romance	no. 1	Jan. 1954	Steriographic Publications
3-D Action	no. 1	Jan. 1954	Animirth Comics/Atlas
3-D Tales of the West	no. 1	Jan. 1954	Canam Publishers/Atlas
True 3-D	no. 2	Feb. 1954	Harvey Publications
Peter Cottontail Three Dimension Comics	no. 1	Feb. 1954	Key Publications
Three Dimension EC Classics	no. 1	1954	I. C. Publishing Co.
Three Dimensional Tales from the Crypt of Terror	no. 2	1954	I. C. Publishing Co.
Mad	no. 12	June 1954	Educational Comics
Batman Adventures in Amazing 3-D Action (reprint)		1966	National Periodical Publications
Deep 3-D Comix	no. 1	1970	Krupp Comic Works

For More Information

For those readers who want to know more about subjects we have touched on in this book, the following list of books, journals, and addresses might be a helpful start.

The best book about 19th-century stereo photography is William C. Darrah's *The World of Stereographs* (1977: William C. Darrah, Publisher, Gettysburg, Pennsylvania) which gives information about the publishers of stereo views and the range of subjects to be found by the collector. The National Stereoscopic Association (Box 14801, Columbus, OH 43214), a stereo organization with a bias toward the collector of old stereo views, publishes a highly informative bimonthly magazine, *Stereo World*. Annual dues to the Association are currently $16 a year. *Stereo World* has included articles in recent months on the history of Tru-Vue and Vectographs, as well as many on various aspects of 19th-century stereographs.

For those who want to take their own 3-D photographs, *Stereo World* runs classified ads that regularly include used stereo cameras, as does *Shutterbug Ads* ($2/issue or $10/year, P.O. Box F, Titusville, FL 32780). There are also camera dealers who specialize in used stereo equipment, among them Ron Speicher (536 Nassau Ave., Freeport, NY 11520), Photography Unlimited (8211 27th Ave., St. Petersburg, FL 33710), Mr. Poster (Box 1883, S. Hackensack, NJ 07606), and Heyderhoff Stereo Supplies (2404 Noyes St., Evanston, IL 60201). Send a stamped, self-addressed envelope for current stock and prices. Mr. Poster also sells a useful illustrated guide to stereo cameras, viewers, projectors, and accessories.

Another very good source of information is Reel 3-D Enterprises (P.O. Box 35, Duarte, CA 91010). They offer bound sets of the no-longer-published *Reel 3-D News*, which is filled with articles about View-Master, stereo projection, stereo cameras, etc. The company also sells reproductions of the handbooks that originally came with the various stereo cameras—very useful items for stereo camera owners. Again, send them a stamped, self-addressed envelope for prices.

If you have a stereo camera and want to improve your stereo technique, two books you might find helpful are: *Tips and Techniques for Better Stereo Pictures* (available from Charles Nims, 5540 Blackstone Ave., Chicago, IL 60637) and *Technical Installments* (available from Charles Piper, 26810 Fond Du Lac Rd., Rancho Palos Verdes, CA 90274). The Stereo Division of the Photographic Society of America is also a helpful organization for the stereo photographer. Write to Steve Traudt (2726 Washington St., Lincoln, NB 68502) for membership information. The International Stereoscopic Union, another stereo organization, publishes a quarterly journal, *Stereoscopy*. For a subscription send your name, address, and the membership dues of $6.50 to Paul Wing (12 Weston Rd., Hingham, MA 02043). One last journal of interest is *3-D International Times* (122 S. Carondelet St., Los Angeles, CA 90057), which can be sent to you monthly for $15 a year.

If you are interested in starting a collection of 3-D comic books, a good first source is Robert M. Overstreet's *Comic Book Price Guide* (published annually: Harmony Books, New York). In addition to listing prices, the book runs advertisements from comic book dealers across the country.

There are a number of books available on the subject of holography, but as a good introduction we recommend Michael Wenyon's *Understanding Holography* (1978: Arco Publishing Co., New York).

Acknowledgments

This book could never have been completed without the help of many people who gave freely of their time and expertise, and who allowed the authors access to their libraries and picture collections. Very special thanks are due to David Starkman and Susan Pinsky for providing numerous illustrations, for helping with difficult copy photography, and for verifying the accuracy of our writing about stereo photography. Special thanks are also due to Andre de Toth, Jack Arnold, John Dennis, Paul Wing, Laurie Phillip, Henry Deeks, Stephen Benton, William Gaines, Joe Kubert, Norman Maurer, Bill Woggon, Sid Jacobson, Howard Nostrand, Marty Epp, Craig Leavitt, Jack Adler, Norman Liss, David Berenson, Tom Thomas, Art Linkletter, and Karen Glass for their generous help with our research for the book; and to Louise and Mary Gunter, Dorothy Wren, Chester Burger, Don and Betty Tucker, Chris Coenen, Mandy Morgan, William Schaeffer, and Geraldine Howard for their help in providing illustrations. For encouragement and help along the way, thanks are due to Barry Lippman, Rick Balkin, Polly Cone, Ellen Morgan, Ken Boege, Walter Weintz, and Caroline Weintz. Our deepest gratitude to Eleanor Caponigro, Don DeHoff, and Gary Gurwitz for their help in getting the project started.

Index

Adam and Six Eves, 158

Adams, Julia, 83, 94

Adventures in 3-D, 123–30, 135

American Colortype, 17, 107

American Sterographic Corporation, 109

Anaglyph: printing, 14, 17, 107, 157–58; projection, 14

Andy Warhol's Frankenstein, 161, 163

A*P*E, 161

Arena, 72

Arnold, Jack, 66, 68, 86, 94, 104

Atlas Comics, 142–44

Audioscopiks, 22, 72

Bandit Island, 77

Bancroft, Ann, 100

Batman, 130, 148, 157

Bayou, 162

Bellboy and the Playgirls, 158–59

Benton, Stephen A., 164

Bolex Stereo Movie camera, 44

Boo Moon, 77

Brewer, Theresa, 84

Britton, Barbara, 54

Bronson, Charles, 58, 91

Brugiére Stéréocartes, 156

The Bubble, 159

Burr, Raymond, 100

Busch Verascope F40 camera, 42

Bwana Devil, 52–57, 163

Calvet, Corinne, 84

Capital Hill Girls, The, 161

Captain 3-D, 130–33, 135

Carey, Phil, 88

Carlson, Richard, 66–68, 72–74, 94

Cat Women of the Moon, 92

Cease Fire, 89

Charge at Feather River, 74–76, 79

Charito and Ernesto, 158

Chrysler Motor Corporation: 3-D film, 22–23

Cinemascope, 78–79, 85, 105, 158

Cinerama, 25, 53–54, 78

Cobb, Lee J., 100

Cole, Michael, 159

Comin' at Ya, 162

Compco Triad stereo projector, 45

Coppola, Francis Ford, 159

Coronet stereo camera, 45

Creature from the Black Lagoon, 92, 94–95

Dahl, Arlene, 71–72

Dangerous Mission, 100, 102

Darnell, Linda, 80–81

David White Company, 32–33, 36–38, 45, 49, 51

Davis, Jack, 145, 147

De Toth, Andre, 56, 61, 63

Deep 3-D Comix, 148, 157

Depth perception: explanation of, 9–10

Devil's Canyon, 79, 82

Dial M for Murder, 100, 103–04, 162

Domo Arigato, 160–61

Dru, Joanne, 82

Drums of Tahiti, 92

Dynasty, 161

Eastman Kodak Company, 14, 45, 49, 155, 162

Eastwood, Clint, 104

E.C. Comics, 144–53

Edixa stereo camera, 49

Eisenhower, Dwight D., 38–41, 50

Elder, Will, 145, 147–53

Euclid, 9

Experiments in Love, 161

Fantastic Invasion of the Planet Earth, 159

Felix the Cat, 135

Ferrer, José, 91

Flaherty, Robert, 54

Fleming, Rhonda, 79, 84

Flesh for Frankenstein, 161

Flight to Tangier, 84–85

Fontaine, Joan, 84

Fort Ti, 64, 68, 76

Frankenstein's Bloody Terror, 160

French Line, The, 96–98

Funk in 3-D, 161

Gabor, Dennis, 163

Gaines, William, 144–45, 147–48

Gance, Able, 17

Glass Web, The, 86

Gog, 100

Gorilla at Large, 100

Grayson, Kathryn, 86–88

Gum cards, 140–41

Gun Fury, 88

Gunzberg, Milton and Julian, 54, 57

Haneel Tri-Vision camera, 43

Hannah Lee, 79, 82

Harvey Publications, 123, 130, 135

Harvey 3-D Hits, 130

Haynes, Roberta, 88

Hayworth, Rita, 91–92

Heflin, Van, 83

Hitchcock, Alfred, 100, 103–04

Hollywood Stereoscopic Society, 36–37

Holography, 163–64

Hondo, 89–91

House of Terror, The, 111, 114, 116–17

House of Wax, 56–65, 78, 160, 162–63

Hudson, Rock, 88, 93

Hurst, Veronica, 72–74

Hypnotic Hick, 77

I, the Jury, 79–80

Iloca camera, 42

In Tune with Tomorrow, 22–23

Indian Warriors, 135

Inferno, 79–80

Ireland, John, 82

It Came from Outer Space, 66–70, 77

Jesse James vs the Daltons, 99, 102

Jet Pup, 135

Jiggs and Maggie, 135

Jivaro, 100

Jules Richard Company, 14, 42

Jungle Thrills, 135

Katy Keene, 135, 139

Katzenjammer Kids, The, 135

Keel, Howard, 86–88

Kelly, Grace, 104

Kin-Dar stereo camera, 49

Kirby, Jack, 130

Kirk, Phyllis, 58–59, 62

Kiss Me Kate, 86, 88

Kodak Stereo camera, 49

Krigstein, Bernard, 145–47

Krupp Comic Works, 157

Kubert, Joe, 107–11, 114, 117–21

Lamas, Fernando, 71–72

Land, Edwin H., 22, 30

Laurie, Piper, 102

Lawrence, Barbara, 102

Lewis, Jerry, 95–96

Linex stereo camera, 49

Linkletter, Art, 36–37

Little Eva, 111

Lloyd, Harold, 36–37

Lovejoy, Frank, 58, 75

Lumberjack Rabbit, 77

Lunacy, 16

Lundigan, William, 79

McDonald's "3-D Happy Meal", 158

MacMurray, Fred, 85

MacyArt Process Corporation, 17, 123

Mad Magician, The, 100–01, 163
Malden, Karl, 99
Magnificent Bodyguards, The, 161
Man in the Dark, 56–57, 64
Marciano-Walcott Fight, 77
Martin, Dean, 95–96
Marvin, Lee, 83, 100
Mask, The, 157–59
Mature, Victor, 102
Maurer, Norman, 107–09, 114, 117–21
Mayo, Virginia, 82
Maze, The, 72–74
Medina, Patricia, 92, 99
Melody, 64–66, 76
Mighty Mouse, 106–09, 130
Miller, Ann, 86–88
Miss Sadie Thompson, 91–92, 163
Mitchell, Cameron, 100
Mitchum, Robert, 80–81
Money from Home, 95–96
Moonlighter, The, 85
Moropticon, 95
Movies of the Future, 15
Napoleon, 17
Nat "King" Cole Sings "Pretend", 76–77
National Comics Publications, 123, 130
National Lampoon, 157–58
Natural Vision, 54, 56–57, 61, 66, 89, 91
Nebraskan, The, 88
New Audioscopiks, 22
New York World's Fair, 1939, 22–25
Nimslo camera, 156–57
North and South Chivalry, The, 161
Nostrand, Howard, 123–24
Nozze Vagabond, 22
Oboler, Arch, 53–54, 56, 159–61
Ouch, 16
Page, Geraldine, 89–90
Palance, Jack, 81, 84
Parasite, 162
Pardon My Backfire, 76–77
Plasticon, 15
Phantom of the Rue Morgue, 99
Plastigrams, 16
Pola-Lite, 95
polarizing filters; explanation of, 22, 30
Polaroid Corporation, 22–23, 30–31, 45, 95, 164
Popeye, Ace of Space, 77
Powell, Bob, 123

Power of Love, The, 15
Price, Vincent, 58, 60–61, 63, 100–02
Projection: single-strip systems, 95
Ray, Aldo, 92
Reed, Donna, 88
Revenge of the Creature, 105
Revere 33 stereo camera, 45, 51
Robinson, Edward G., 86
Robot Monster, 72, 75
Roland, Gilbert, 97–98
Runaway Taxi, A, 16
Rush, Barbara, 66–68
Russell, Jane, 96–98
Ryan, Robert, 79
St. John Publishing Company, 107–09, 111, 114, 117, 123, 130
Sangaree, 71–72
Sawyer's, Inc., 25–29, 43–44, 155
Scott, Randolph, 83
Sea Dream, 162
Second Chance, 79–81
Secrets of Ecstasy '72, The, 160
Seduction of the Innocent, 144, 148
Seein' is Believin', 162
September Storm, 158
Sesame Street's Big Bird 3-D viewer, 156
Sheena the Jungle Queen, 135, 138
Smith, Pete, 22–23
Southwest Passage, 100
Space Attack, 158
Spooks, 76, 163
Stack, Robert, 54
Stanwyck, Barbara, 85
Starlets, The, 161
Stereo Brownie camera, 15
Stereo Realist camera, 32–43, 45, 51, 155
Stereo Realist ST 42 camera, 42
Stereo Realist projector, 42
Stereo slide viewers, 45, 49, 51
Stereoscopics, 16
Stereoscope, 10–13
Stereo-Tach, 33
Stereo 35 camera, 156
Steriographic Publications, 135
Stewardesses, The, 160
Stranger Wore a Gun, The, 79, 83
Super Realist stereo camera, 49
Superman, 122–23, 130
Surf!!, 162
Swing Tail, 160

Tarzan, 140–41
Taza, Son of Cochise, 92–95
TDC Stereo Colorist camera, 49
TDC Stereo Vivid camera, 49
TDC Stereo Vivid projector, 42
Teleview, 15–16
Third Dimension Murder, 23
13 Ghosts, 158
13 Nuns, 161
Those Redheads from Seattle, 84–85
3-D Action, 143
3-D Dolly, 130
3-D glasses, 14, 23, 148, 157
3-D Illustereo Process, 109, 123
3-D Love, 134–37
3-D Romance, 135
3-D Tales of the West, 142
3-D television, 163
3-D Video Corporation, 163
Three-Dimensional E.C. Classics, 144, 146–47
Three Dimensional Tales from the Crypt of Terror, 144–45
Three Dimensions of Greta, The, 160
Three Stooges, The, 76–77, 108–09, 111, 114–15, 123
Tor, 108–14
True 3-D, 130, 135
True 3-D processes, 123–24
Tru-Vue, 18–21, 25, 43–44, 108
Vectograph, 30–31, 95
Verascope, 14, 42
Videon Stereo camera, 42–43, 49
Videon II stereo camera, 45
View-Master, 25–29, 43–44, 154–56; Mark II camera, 155; Personal stereo camera, 43; Stereomatic 500 projector, 44
Waller, Fred, 25, 53
Wayne, John, 89–90
Whack, 111, 117–21
Whitney, Peter, 100
Wilson, Gahan, 158
Wings of the Hawk, 79, 83
Winpro stereo camera, 45
Wollensak Stereo 10 camera, 49
Working for Peanuts, 66
Zowie, 16
Zum Greifen Nah, 22

The Authors

Hal Morgan is the author of *Big Time: American Tall-Tale Postcards* and a coauthor of *Prairie Fires and Paper Moons: The American Photographic Postcard, 1900–1920*. He works as a book designer and producer in Cambridge, Massachusetts. (1956 photo)

Dan Symmes has been obsessed with 3-D since he read his first 3-D comic book as a child. He currently works as Vice President and Technical Director of 3-D Video Corp. in Los Angeles. He has worked in various capacities on more than sixteen 3-D films since 1970.